What People Are Saying About
Chicken Soup for the
Mother o

"Every now and the ⬚⬚⬚⬚⬚⬚⬚⬚⬚ life that allows them to refocus ⬚⬚⬚⬚⬚⬚⬚⬚ at come with parenting a preschooler. *Chicken Soup for the Mother of Preschooler's Soul* is like a latte for the mind."

—**Maria Bailey**
Founder of BlueSuitMom.com and host, Mom Talk Radio

"Of all the things a mom with preschoolers needs—a bit of laughter and encouragement. The stories in *Chicken Soup for the Mother of Preschooler's Soul* will not only refresh moms, but also remind her of the precious gift she is to her children."

Lisa Whelchel
actress; author of the bestseller, Creative Correction; founder of www.MomTime.com

"Every preschooler mom would be blessed to steal away to a comfy place and be filled up by this wonderful book. Each witty entry made me laugh, relate, reflect and rejoice. Each page of *Chicken Soup for the Mother of Preschooler's Soul* contains wonderfully written, poignant reminders that we are not alone in this adventure, and we are truly blessed to be called 'Mommy.'"

—**Jana Alayra**
worship leader/recording artist for children

"*Chicken Soup for the Mother of Preschooler's Soul* takes you on a mom's journey through the preschool years. You'll find yourself cheering with a mom's moment of success, laugh with her in the midst of chaos and delighting in those oh so precious moments. Wonderfully written, these stories are guaranteed to change your heart."

—**Twila C. Liggett, Ph.D.**
executive producer & founder
Reading Rainbow

"*Chicken Soup for the Mother of Preschooler's Soul* is the perfect remedy for those chaotic times in a mom's busy day. The stories will certainly touch all moms and remind them how much mothering matters."

—**Karol Ladd**
author of *The Power of a Positive Mom*
www.PositiveMom.com

"*Chicken Soup for the Mother of Preschooler's Soul* is the perfect pick-me-up for those down-and-out days when your little one stages a temper tantrum on the kitchen floor— just as the doorbell rings. Each story will make you feel better than eating an entire bag of the kids' cookies, calling a friend and having a good cry rolled into one. Drop the kids off at preschool and relax with a little Chicken Soup."

—**Jen Singer**
creator *www.MommaSaid.net*
author, *14 Hours 'Til Bedtime*

"This is a great book! Moms with little ones need constant reminders that the events wearing them out today will be the stories they'll share with anyone who'll listen later. When our kids are grown and gone, there is no period of time that we'll long for more!"

—**Kelly McCausey**
host, Work at Home Moms Talk Radio

"As a mother of two boys, one of whom is a preschooler, I can relate to the antics and heartwarming stories.

Chicken Soup for the Mother of Preschooler's Soul captures the essence of real life and allows moms to relate their own stories, as we all have many of our own to share!"

—**Tara Paterson**
founder *JustForMom.com* and the
Just For Mom Foundation

"Tender hearts, disarming honesty and surprising wisdom. Preschool children have these qualities in abundance, but they are often overlooked in the hectic pace of day-to-day life. *Chicken Soup for the Mother of Preschooler's Soul* is a collection of simple, breathtaking stories of motherhood that will remind busy moms to slow down and enjoy each precious moment with their children."

—**Suzanne Hadley**
children's editor

CHICKEN SOUP FOR THE MOTHER OF PRESCHOOLER'S SOUL

Stories to Refresh and Rekindle the Spirit of Moms of Little Ones

Jack Canfield
Mark Victor Hansen
Maria Nickless, Elisa Morgan
with Carol McAdoo Rehme

Health Communications, Inc.
Deerfield Beach, Florida

www.hcibooks.com
www.chickensoup.com

We would like to acknowledge the following publishers and individuals for permission to reprint the following material. (Note: The stories that were written by Jack Canfield, Mark Victor Hansen or Maria Nickless are not included in this listing.)

Time Well Spent. Reprinted by permission of Cheryl Kirking. ©1999 Cheryl Kirking.

Copycat. Reprinted by permission of Karin A. Lovold. ©2003 Karin A. Lovold.

Remembering Mama. Reprinted by permission of Mimi Greenwood Knight. ©1998 Mimi Greenwood Knight.

On Parade. Reprinted by permission of Mimi Greenwood Knight. ©2001 Mimi Greenwood Knight.

Sorting It Out. Reprinted by permission of Angela Gail Barr. ©2005 Angela Gail Barr.

(Continued on page 271)

Publisher: Health Communications, Inc.
       3201 S.W. 15th Street
       Deerfield Beach, FL 33442–8190

Cover design by Andrea Perrine Brower
Inside formatting by Dawn Von Strolley Grove

This book is dedicated to our children, Madison and Jack Nickless, and Eva and Ethan Morgan. Thanks for creating all those priceless moments that taught us how to be your moms. We love you.

Contents

Acknowledgments xv

Foreword xix

Introduction xxi

Share with Us xxiii

1. MOTHERING MATTERS

Time Well Spent *Cheryl Kirking* 2

Copycat *Karin A. Lovold* 5

Remembering Mama *Mimi Greenwood Knight* 7

On Parade *Mimi Greenwood Knight* 10

Sorting It Out *Angie Barr* 13

Obstacles and Opportunities *Karna Converse* 15

Working It Out *Gloria Wooldridge* 18

A Window to Look Through *Brian G. Jett* 20

2. MOM'S LOVE

You Might Be a Mommy If . . . *Leslie Wilson* 25

Bedtime Miracle *Bonnie Compton Hanson* 27

Flannel in the Food Court *Emily Okaty Wilson* 28

Promises, Promises *Christine M. Smith* 32

In His Second Year *Michele Ivy Davis* 34

Without Words *Diane Kagey* 36

Career-Minded *Maria Nickless* 39

Purple Principles *Maureen Johnson* 42

The House That Mommy Built *Maryjo Faith Morgan* 46

Hair Today *Amanda L. Stevens* 49

Mothering: The Next Generation *Sally Friedman* 51

3. INSIGHTS AND LESSONS

Food for Thought *Lisa Wood Curry* 56

On the Table *Lizann Flatt* 60

Blown Away *Kristin Walker* 63

The Potty Predicament *Jackie Papandrew* 66

The Green One *June Williams* 70

Through the Looking Glass *Lisa Moffitt* 74

The Critter Brigade *Mimi Greenwood Knight* 76

The Storyteller *Eliza Ong* 79

The Little Things *Amy Krause* 81

4. A MATTER OF PERSPECTIVE: BUILDING BLOCKS

Lucky Me *Sheri Plucker* 84

One Day, Some Day *Lisa Moffitt* 86

Taking Account *Cindy Gehl* 88

On the Run *Renee Hixson* 91

Play-Doh Perfection *Sandra Giordano* 96

Wishful Thinking *Donna Lowich* 100

Wheels *Sheree Rochelle Gaudet* 102

5. LAUGHTER IN THE CHAOS

Red-Faced and Remembering *Mindy Ferguson* 107

The Race *Natalie Bright*..109

When It Rains, It Pours *Maria Monto* 112

Market Madness *Caroline Akervik* 116

Mr. Clean *Rita M. Pilger* 119

Story Time *Sherrie Peterson* 121

Taming Temper Tantrums *Kay Conner Pliszka*....................................123

Gunning for Perfection *Rochelle Nelson* 126

A Higher Perspective *Jennifer Oscar* 128

6. TIME OUT!

"Be" Is for Bunko *Tessa Floehr* 135

We Interrupt This Parent *Mimi Greenwood Knight*.............................137

Down and Out *Linda C. Apple*..140

It's All in the Timing *Stephen D. Rogers*..142

Rosie's Salon *Myrna C. G. Mibus*...145

Pavement Paradise *Rachelle Hughes* 148

On a Role *Linda Vujnov*...150

The Sound of Silence *Mandy Flynn* 152

7. HELPING HANDS

Seasonal Secrets *Sandra Byrd*..156

Hand and Heart *Elaine L. Bridge*..159

Holding On *Cheryl Kirking*...161

A Little Help Please *Libby Hempen*..163

Daddy Bear *Melissa Blanco* 167

Oh, What a Ride! *Sally Friedman* 171

Bee Attitude *Andrea Stark*..173

Bearing Thanksgiving *Jaye Lewis*...176

8. THROUGH THE EYES OF A CHILD

Of Two Minds *Carol McAdoo Rehme* 180

Meeting Jeanie *Tanya Lentz* 182

The Grill Drill *Jennifer Brown* 184

Spiced Up *Marilyn G. Nutter* 187

When I'm a Grown-Up *Jodi Seidler* 190

Cents and Sensitivity *Tasha Jacobson* 192

Picking and Choosing *Jennifer Lawler* 195

9. LET SCHOOL BEGIN

Marker Magic *Kathleen Ahrens, Ph.D., and Tracy Love, Ph.D.* 200

Back-to-School Q&A *Sarah Smiley* 203

Growing Up *Marsha B. Smith* 206

Preschool Pangs *Kristine Yankee* 209

Fears and Tears *Libby Kennedy* 212

Late Bloomers *Cheryl L. Butler* 216

Mommy's Help, Er *Patricia E. Van West* 219

Special Delivery *Carita S. Barlow* 222

Hire Calling *Avagail Burton* 225

10. PRECIOUS MOMENTS

The Mom *Maria Nickless* 228

Rainy Day Cake *Mary Comeau-Kronenwetter* 231

Superheroes *Christina Quist* 233

At Your Service *Tsgoyna Tanzman* 236

All That Glitters *Stephanie Ray Brown* 239

X-Ray Vision *Jo Moon* 242

Paying the Price *Autumn Conley* 245

A Higher Plane *Ellen Javernick* 248

Cookie Cutter Connection *Tessa Floehr* 250

Weavings *Karen Olson Burkhartzmeyer* 252

More Chicken Soup? 255

Supporting Mothers of Preschoolers Around the World 256

Who Is Jack Canfield? 257

Who Is Mark Victor Hansen? 258

Who Is Maria Nickless? 259

Who Is Elisa Morgan? 260

Contributors 261

Permissions *(continued)* 271

Acknowledgments

We wish to express our heartfelt gratitude to the following people who helped make this book possible:

Our families, who have been chicken soup for our souls!

Jack's family—Inga, Travis, Riley, Christopher, Oran and Kyle—for all their love and support.

Mark's family—Patty, Elisabeth and Melanie—for once again sharing and lovingly supporting us in creating yet another book.

Maria's husband, Ward, for your generous love and faithfulness, and all you do to support my dreams. I love you. Madison and Jack, for blessing me with the title of Mommy—you are my treasures stored in heaven.

Maria's mother, Eileen, thanks for being a great example. And to all my mommy friends—especially Linda Yates, Jennifer Briner and Jenny Smith—thank you for all your prayers and encouragement along the way. Finally, thanks to Gina Romanello, for always being there to help me—you rock, my friend!

Elisa's family—Evan, Ethan, Eva and Marcus—much love and thanks! Also, many thanks to all the zillions of MOPS moms who have either submitted a story for this book or lived one out in real life. You are the heroes!

Carol McAdoo Rehme, once again you've breathed life

into the stories. You are brilliant with words! Thank you for your incredible gift of editing and endearing friendship. We could not have done it without you.

Beth Lagerborg and Rachel Ryan, much love and thanks for all the help you provided in so many ways.

Our publisher, Peter Vegso, for his vision and commitment to bringing *Chicken Soup for the Soul* to the world.

Patty Aubery and Russ Kamalski, for being there on every step of the journey, with love, laughter and endless creativity.

D'ette Corona, for always having an armor of knowledge and a shield of calmness to guide us through the process.

Patty Hansen, for your thorough and competent handling of the legal and licensing aspects of the *Chicken Soup for the Soul* books. You are magnificent at the challenge!

Veronica Romero, Teresa Esparza, Barbara Lomonaco, Robin Yerian, Jesse Ianniello, Laren Edlestein, Laurie Hartman, Jody Emme, Debbie Lefever, Michelle Adams, Dee Dee Romanello, Shanna Vieyra, Lisa Williams, Gina Romanello, Brittany Shaw, Dena Jacobson, Tanya Jones and Mary McKay, who support Jack's and Mark's businesses with skill and love.

Allison Janse, for editing our final manuscript. Thank you once again for being there whenever we need you.

Bret Witter, Elisabeth Rinaldi and Kathy Grant, our editors at Health Communications, Inc., for their devotion to excellence.

Terry Burke, Lori Golden, Kelly Maragni, Sean Geary, Patricia McConnell, Ariana Daner, Kim Weiss, Paola Fernandez-Rana, and the entire sales, marketing and PR departments at Health Communications, Inc., for doing such an incredible job of supporting our books.

Tom Sand, Claude Choquette and Luc Jutras, who manage year after year to get our books translated into thirty-six languages around the world.

The art department at Health Communications, Inc., for their talent, creativity and unrelenting patience in producing book covers and inside designs that capture the essence of Chicken Soup: Larissa Hise Henoch, Lawna Patterson Oldfield, Andrea Perrine Brower, Anthony Clausi, Kevin Stawieray and Dawn Von Strolley Grove.

All the *Chicken Soup for the Soul* coauthors, who make it such a joy to be part of this *Chicken Soup* family.

Our glorious panel of readers who helped us make the final selections and made invaluable suggestions on how to improve the book: Dale Bendsak, Michelle Blank, Jennifer Brown, Julie Cantrell, Denise Carr, Sharon Castiglione, Pat Cavallin, Cheryl Cazer, Crystal Clark, Amy Colella, Helen Colella, John Cox, Edie Cuttler, Christine Dahl, Gloria Dahl, Mary Damask, Michelle Dickson, Janine Durbin, Pat Evans, Peg Frezon, Courtney Gillett, Nancy Hadley, Cindy Hoffman, Diane Kagey, Barbara LoMonaco, Mona Marushak, Dawn McCrory, Nicola Mingins, Lisa Mitchum, Michelle Newell, Eliza Ong, Naomi Overton, Tyler Overton, Patti Penrod, Joyce Rapier, Nicole Romero, Kimberly Ryan, J.J. Smith, Jean Stewart, B. J. Taylor, Stephanie Thompson, Beth VanMeurs, Laurie Walker and Colleen Williams.

And, most of all, thanks to everyone who submitted their heartfelt stories, poems, quotes and cartoons for possible inclusion in this book. While we were not able to use everything you sent in, we know that each word came from a magical place flourishing within your souls.

Because of the size of this project, we may have left out the names of some people who contributed along the way. If so, we are sorry, but please know that we really do appreciate you very much. We are truly grateful and love you all!

Foreword

Dear Mom of Preschoolers,

Back when my now-grown children were teensy, I learned a wonderful lesson in mothering: Celebrate the good moments. The thrown-together supper that they christened "the best meal in the world!" My automatic "sure" when they begged for ice cream mid-errands. My decision to pause for lap-reading in spite of endless, seemingly important tasks demanding my attention.

But, hey, I've had my fair share of less-than-perfect mommy moments.

"No more uppies! Mommy's tired," I've sighed.

"How come nobody ever gives Mommy kisses anymore?" I've whined.

"Go play by yourself. Mommy's too busy right now," I've grouched.

At MOPS International, we often say a mother of preschoolers is like a cardboard juice box—with umpteen straws stuck inside. Her little ones gulp and gulp until she feels sucked dry.

The task of mothering well is possible when we mother strategically. When we invest in ourselves as moms, we're more capable of investing in our children. The book in your hands, *Chicken Soup for the Mother of Preschooler's Soul,* will nourish you with its stories of challenge, humor and hope. As you read, you'll applaud the good mommy moments and gain perspective from those less-than-perfect examples.

Today makes a difference tomorrow. Mothering preschoolers is a short interlude on the parenting calendar, but it's full of countless opportunities. Let's celebrate them together!

Elisa Morgan
President and CEO
MOPS International

Introduction

You work endlessly from morning till dusk. You are head cook and chief taxi driver. You are the keeper of the Cheerios, the dream maker and the boo-boo healer. As a master multi-tasker, you clean house, do laundry and make lunch—all while maintaining a character role in your child's game of make-believe. You are a master educator with an answer for every "why?" With superhero power, you accomplish the unimaginable—even with a little one strapped to your leg whining, "Up, Mommy."

Yet, in the midst of your busyness, you find time to cuddle and kiss and relish the affection of your children.

This book is our gift to you: for all those months that seem endless, those days you feel disappointment or confusion, and those moments when you wonder—"Is mothering supposed to look like this?" We hope this book helps bridge the gap between unrealistic expectations and the undeniable reality of a mom's day-to-day life.

Within these stories, you'll discover significance in your mothering, balance and laughter in your chaos, and a new language of love for your children. You'll learn that your daily presence *is* your child's present. You'll find that help is there for the asking . . . and so is time for yourself. You'll laugh at life from a child's perspective. You'll wince at the pain of letting them go as they enter school for the first time. And you'll learn that, although the days might seem too long, the years will be too short.

So, with deep love and respect for all you do, we offer *Chicken Soup for the Mother of Preschooler's Soul*. Let it refresh your soul and rekindle your spirit.

Share with Us

We would like to invite you to send us stories you would like to see published in future editions of *Chicken Soup for the Soul*.

We would also love to hear your reactions to the stories in this book. Please let us know what your favorite stories are and how they affected you.

Please submit your stories on our Web site:

www.chickensoup.com

Chicken Soup for the Soul
P.O. Box 30880
Santa Barbara, CA 93130
fax: 805-563-2945

We hope you enjoy reading this book as much as we enjoyed compiling, editing and writing it.

Reprinted by permission of Jonny Hawkins. ©2005.

1

MOTHERING MATTERS

The art of mothering is to teach the art of living to children.

Elain Heffner

Time Well Spent

Begin with the end in mind.

Stephen Covey

Are you a mother? Do you ever wonder
   if you accomplish much each day?
When you see the floor that didn't get mopped
   or the laundry still not put away?
If you sometimes feel discouraged,
   I've a few questions to ask of you.
Perhaps it's time to take a look at all the things you do.

Did you fold a paper airplane?
   Did you wash a sticky face?
Did you help your child pick up toys
   and put them in their place?
Did you pull a wagon, push a swing
   or build a blanket tent?
If so, let me tell you that your day was quite well spent.

Did you turn the TV off and send
   the children out to play?

And then watch them from the window
  as you prayed about their day?
When they tracked mud on your kitchen floor,
  did you try hard not to scold?
Did you snuggle close as prayers were said
  and bedtime stories told?

Did you wipe away a tear?
  Did you pat a little head?
Did you kiss a tender cheek
  as you tucked your child in bed?
Did you thank God for your blessings,
  for your children heaven-sent?
Then rest assured, dear mother,
  your time was quite well spent.

Did you make sure they brushed their teeth today?
  Did you comb tangles from her hair?
Did you tell them they should do what's right,
  though life's not always fair?
Did you quiz her on her spelling words,
  as you tried hard not to yawn?
Did you marvel at how tall he is
  and wonder where his childhood's gone?

Did buy another gallon of milk?
  Was that broccoli you cooked?
Did you straighten your son's tie and say
  how handsome he looked?
Did you hold your tearful daughter
  when her teenage heart was broken?
Did you help her find some peace of mind,
  although few words were spoken?

Did you help him choose a college
   and get the applications sent?
Did you feel a little wistful
   at how quickly the years went?
Did you help her pack a suitcase
   and try hard not to cry?
Did you bravely smile and smooth her hair
   as you hugged her good-bye?

Do you hold them in your prayers although
   your arms must let them go?
Do you tell them that you love them,
   so they will always know?
To make a home where love abides
   is a great accomplishment
And to serve God as a mother is
   to live a life well spent.

Cheryl Kirking

Copycat

Like mother, like daughter.

English Proverb

My little Brittany wants to be like me. How scary is that?

The other day she watched me brush my teeth. A few nights later, she darted out of the bathroom with a wide, pearly-white grin. "I can brush my teeth just like you!"

"Oh, that's nice, dear." My response was casual.

"I even spit like you, too!" My head shot up as she vanished from my room.

Can I stand the pressure of this?

When I lean into the mirror to put on mascara, she leans in, too, and I feel her eyes on me. When I sing in the kitchen, she memorizes the words, and the next time she sings it with me. When I talk, she hangs on every word I say, every expression I utter, and I know she'll repeat it all some day—in the exact tone of voice.

What an opportunity!

With her little eyes watching me, examining me and learning from me, I long to be my best, to live my best. To be a good example. To be the kind of person who merits mimicking. No words teach as powerfully as my actions. What I do and say, how I do it and say it . . . Brittany is there. Aware. Ready to copy me. Wanting to *be like me.*

So, for now, it's okay if she studies me—how I brush my teeth, put on mascara or sing a song. If she's watching the little things, then I know she's watching the big things. The important things. The traits and characteristics I hope to instill in her life, too.

How awesome is that?

Karin A. Lovold

Remembering Mama

Remember when we were teenagers and our parents were idiots? They knew nothing about fashion, music, hairstyles or anything else that was important.

To paraphrase Mark Twain, it's amazing how much smarter my mother seems now that I'm older myself. Since my oldest daughter was born seven years ago, my mother has gotten progressively more intelligent in my eyes. Unfortunately, she died almost ten years before I had my first child, so I can't tell her just how wise I now realize she was.

My mother raised twelve kids. But, as anyone from a large family can attest, there were always many more than that playing in the backyard, eating around the dinner table—even, it seemed to me, in the bathtub. A few cousins were spending the summer. Someone's parents were going through a divorce. Someone else's family moved away, and the kids were finishing out the school year with us. Yet there was always enough food on the table and enough of her time to go around. (Mama used to say that you don't divide your love; you multiply it.)

My mother never raised her voice. This is not an exaggeration; it is a fact. I never really appreciated the self-control this must have taken until I had my own houseful. I have to admit, there are days when I hear a screaming maniac in my house and realize it's me. How did she do it? And why didn't I inherit her peaceful nature?

Mama sang all the time. She sang in the kitchen. She sang in the car. She sang when she asked you to do something. I can hear her now: "Michelle, please empty the dishwasher; Denise, please sweep the kitchen"—all to the tune of "A Tisket, a Tasket." Anytime she was on the brink of losing her temper, I realized, she broke into song— sometimes chanting through clenched teeth, "Leave your little sister alone. I'm not going to ask you again"—this to the tune of "Mary Had a Little Lamb."

In the grocery store the other day, I hung at the end of my rope when, suddenly, I heard myself singing, "We're almost finished. Then we're going home." (The tune was unrecognizable. I inherited a wee bit of Mama's patience, but none of her tunefulness.)

During her forty years raising children, Mama acquired some unbelievable tricks of the trade. Whenever she wanted to introduce a new food, she would serve it in a small casserole dish and announce, "This is a little something I fixed for your dad. If you'd like to try some, you may take a little on your plate. But you don't have to."

Of course, we'd all scramble for it and clean the plate. Dad was lucky to get any at all. Then she'd wait a couple of weeks and serve it again, but in her usual large portions. Someone would exclaim, "Wow, zucchini for everyone!" After that, it became a family favorite.

Hanging on the wall of our kitchen was a chalkboard on which my mother wrote her thought for the day—usually religious, always inspirational. The children in the neighborhood took to cutting through our kitchen on their way to the bus stop in the morning to read it. A few of them, after they went off to college or got married and moved away, would even call from time to time to have it read to them over the phone.

I tried my own thought-for-the-day board. It hung on the fridge—for about a month. I remembered to change the thought—for the first five days. Then the board hung there, with the same thought half-erased, for the next twenty-five days—right next to the behavior charts I had forgotten to keep up with. I've decided to try it again— when the kids are old enough to read.

Yes, she was an incredible woman, my mother. Though I often feel I fall miserably short when I compare my mothering to hers, it gives me great comfort to know that her gentle spirit is within me somewhere. I'm sure it will make itself known—especially when I introduce zucchini to my children.

Mimi Greenwood Knight

On Parade

Her children rise up and bless her.

Proverbs 31:28

"Daddy's home!"

Tiny figures stampede past, each clamoring to get the first hug, the first kiss, all squawking at once.

"I want a piggyback ride!"

"Look what I made for you!"

"Did you bring us anything?"

Daddy throws his arms wide and draws three squirming bodies off the floor. Squeals and giggles abound as he spins them around, returns them to the floor and starts chasing them in every direction.

No more quiet house. No more bathtime. No more Mama. It's as if I've disappeared into the woodwork I've been trying to find time to clean.

He deserves this, I tell myself. *He works extra hard so I can stay home with the kids. This is his reward after a long day at the office.*

Who am I kidding? It hurts to see them shower affection on David, after I've been here, all day long, changing diapers, wiping noses and mopping spills. I'm the one who's not allowed to have a complete thought, stay seated through a meal or enjoy an uninterrupted phone conversation.

I'm in charge of work, worry and discipline; he's in charge of fun, frolic and fantasy. I'm the maid, the cook, the school marm—and the policeman; he's the grand marshal of the nightly daddy parade.

Where's my parade?

Of course, we made this decision together, putting my career on hold to be here for the kids. I never doubted it was the right choice for us, and I still don't. At times, however, it's hard to watch David shower, dress and disappear while I stay home, as steady and loyal as a lap dog.

Just once, I'd like to walk in the door to shouts of "Mommy's home!"

I know I'm being silly. Think of the things he misses out on, things I wouldn't trade for the most glamorous job on the planet. He wasn't here for Molly's first joke, when at a year old she reached into a basket of toys, pulled out a dumbbell-shaped rattle and held it across the bridge of her nose like Mommy's glasses. He didn't hear her belly laugh then or mine when Hewson at two strode through the back door naked except for a pair of muddy rubber boots— smiling ear-to-ear—to hand me a bouquet of ragweed.

He's not here when Molly hurts herself, and before I can reach her, Haley has rushed over to console her. Or when I offer Hewson a cookie, and he won't accept it unless I give him one for each of his "sissies" as well.

I can hear the Daddy Fan Club in the bedroom, fighting over who gets to put his shoes in the closet and who may toss his shirt in the hamper. I don't see anyone wrestling me for my dishrag. But as I clear the table for dinner, I catch glimpses of our day together—masks we constructed from paper plates, flowers plucked on our morning walk, a mountain of library books because we had to have just one more.

Would I trade all of that for a paycheck and a little office camaraderie?

As the daddy procession heads back my way, I have to admit the trade-offs are worth it. He may have lunch out with coworkers, but I get peanut-butter-and-jelly kisses. He might exchange clever repartee with clients, but I get to snuggle up and read *Good Night, Moon* "just one more time."

Let him have his parade. I'll celebrate each day's small joys.

After all, those are perks no benefits package can offer.

Mimi Greenwood Knight

Sorting It Out

Some sort of silent trade takes place between mothers and children.

Yuko Tsushima

It's a day of doing laundry,
A normal daily chore.
Washing, folding, put-a-way
And picking up the floor.

My toddler's running all about,
A ribbon in her hair,
Wearing the cutest little dress
With fashion and with flair.

I venture to the dryer
To switch another batch.
My mouth drops open wide
When I open up the hatch.

The *one* bra I have left to wear
That's nearly a decade old

Looks like it's been rolled around
In some yucky, greenish mold.

Somehow it got sorted in
With all my darks and blues
And now is spotted pink and green
Like smelly bowling shoes.

I just want to sit and sob
When my toddler saunters in
Dressed in too-pricey clothing
And an I-know-I'm-cute grin.

And I realize, right then and there,
How mothering's meant to be.
So I'll wear my ugly, tie-dyed bra
'Cause it's no longer just about me.

Angie Barr

Obstacles and Opportunities

My mother had a great deal of trouble with me, but I think she enjoyed it.

Mark Twain

Dear Ellen,

Last night, you asked if it was hard to be a mom. At that particular time, I was rushing to get dinner on the table, one ear tuned in to you, the other tuned in to the argument that was brewing between your brothers in the basement.

I sighed and hurriedly answered, "Yes, sometimes it is, but it's all worth it. Now go find something to do."

My answer was rushed and a bit flippant, but you were satisfied.

"Good," you said, "'cause I want to be a mom when I grow up." Then, with a big smile, you skipped off to join the noise in the basement.

After you went to bed, I thought a bit more about your question and my answer. And yes, being a mom is hard work. In fact, sometimes it's downright difficult.

I have only a few short years (although sometimes the days seem like eternity) to teach you that you should cross the street at the corner and wear a helmet when you ride your bicycle. That it's right to say "thank you," but wrong to talk to strangers. That it's right to answer the phone, but wrong to say, "My mom's not home."

Being a mom means being a protector, organizer, juggler, chief cook and bottle washer. Some days, the list is never-ending, the responsibility enormous. But every day, I make a choice about how I view my job: a day laden with obstacles to be overcome or one that is brimming with opportunities to be seized.

It's easy to see the obstacles.

White woodwork pocked with black fingerprints. Stains on the carpet. Cobwebs in the corners. Dust bunnies under the beds. Toys on the stairs. Smelly trash. Runny noses. Ratty hair. Holey socks. Wasted food.

When the obstacles are overwhelming, my days are disjointed and tear-stained. These are the days I wear old clothes because, if the baby isn't spitting up on them, the toddler is spilling paint on them. The days when, just as I fall exhausted into bed, a voice calls out from down the hall, "Mom, I wet the bed."

But when I look for the opportunities, I find that I am surrounded.

A warm burp and soft head burrowing into my shoulder. A tent constructed over the dining-room table. An announcement that the art gallery is open and paintings by an accomplished four-year-old can be purchased for a mere five cents. A secret discussion in the basement on the best tactic to use when spying on Mom. A middle-of-the-night poke in the arm with an innocent, "Can I sleep with you?"

I can laugh at your chocolate-moustached faces because I know you like brownies best when they're warm from the oven. I can smile at the soaking wet mittens because I know you're proud of the snow fort you built in the backyard. My days are filled with pep talks of encouragement: Yes, I can get up in the middle of the night, one more time, to nurse the baby—he smells so good. Yes, I can read *The Cat in the Hat* one more time—she still fits on my lap. Yes, I can listen to one more argument and name-calling session without losing my cool—I know someday they'll be best buddies.

Last night, when dinner was over, the three of you ran off with extravagant plans to build a Lego castle that promised to be the biggest one yet. The argument so important before dinner was forgotten. Later, you scrunched newspapers and carried firewood into the house.

"We need lots of wood," you informed me, "because we're going to have a big, big fire." Then you plopped down on the couch and announced, "Listen to me read *Green Eggs and Ham.*"

I heard firewood crackling in the background. I saw swirls of dust through the flames. And I knew that the opportunities of being a mom far outweigh the obstacles.

Is it hard to be a mom? Sometimes.

Is it worth it? Always.

Love, Mom

Karna Converse

Working It Out

*My mother is a poem I'll never be able to write,
though everything I write is a poem to my mother.*

Sharon Doubiago

Everyone experiences them—one of *those* weeks when it seems that every step you take places you two steps behind. Finding myself at a low point and particularly discouraged, I wondered if it was time to re-enter the work force. Time to get out of the house.

Because I'd chosen to be a stay-at-home mom for several years, I waged an internal battle. Would I be able to re-enter the workforce if I waited longer? Would my skills be outdated? Was what I do at home *really* important? Did I even matter?

The following Sunday was Mother's Day. Still feeling down, I slouched in the back row of the church, next to my daughters. As part of the service, our pastor invited the younger children to the front of the sanctuary. Our little Jenny, four years old, joined them.

After speaking a few minutes, the pastor asked the kids what they'd like to be when they grew up. Enthusiastic hands shot into the air. Eager answers abounded.

"A fireman."

"A teacher."

"A doctor."

"A hero."

"President!"

He positioned the microphone in front of Jenny. "And how about you? What do you want to be?"

I held my breath, never certain what our blonde dynamo would come out with.

"When I grow up," her sweet voice was clear, "I want to be . . . a mother."

Silence reigned for a fraction of a moment, and then the congregation chuckled. Our pastor recovered from his surprise. "That's a great choice, Jenny."

No one noticed this mommy in the back row dabbing away her tears. I had arrived at church service unsettled, uncertain and filled with discontent. But I left in peace, finding joy in the confidence that for now, I was doing exactly what I was called to do.

Gloria Wooldridge

A Window to Look Through

Making the decision to have a child—it's momentous. It is to decide forever to have your heart go walking around outside your body.

Elizabeth Stone

She watches through her window, her little girl at play;
Memories flood back to her childhood, of her yesterdays.

As she tucks her gift into bed and kisses her precious face,
She says a prayer of protection, "Lord, keep my child safe."

And as days turn months into years, she sees her little girl
    grow,
And begins to realize that a time will come, the time when
    she must let go.

Suddenly, she hears a gentle voice saying, "No greater
    love is this,
Than what you've done for your little girl; go seal it with a
    kiss."

"Honey, I want to kiss your face, but I know I can't by
   phone.
While looking through your bedroom window, I began to
   feel alone.

"So many days through this very window, I watched you
   laugh and play,
And I can almost see you tucked in bed, the nights we
   talked and prayed."

"Mom," her daughter uttered, "there's something I want to
   say.
You may not know how many times, I saw you watch me
   play.

"That window that you're looking through is the same one
   God looked in.
He saw you by my bed each night when you'd tenderly
   tuck me in.

"So, Mom, please don't feel all alone, you know I'll always
   be there. . . .
Just like God is with you now, no matter the time or place
   or where."

Her mother paused and then replied, "Sweetheart, I know
   you're right.
You're grown, married and have a child that you now tuck
   in at night."

"Mom, I better go now; I have some things I better do."
Her mom replied, "I know it, dear, you've got a window to
   look through."

Brian G. Jett

2

MOM'S LOVE

One word frees us of all the weight and pain of life: That word is love.

Sophocles

© 2005 Jonny Hawkins

You Might Be a Mommy If . . .

Every shirt you own has spit-up on the shoulder.
Must-see TV includes Barney, Arthur and Disney Playhouse.
You carry a diaper bag instead of a purse.
You analyze babies' bodily functions with women you just met.
"Sleeping in" is when the clock reads 6:30 A.M.
You never go anywhere without baby wipes.
You sleep with a baby monitor a foot away from your head.
With each subsequent child, you've progressed from sterilizing the pacifier to washing it off to blowing on it, invoking the three-second rule.
Your children are better dressed than you.
You used to be known by your first name—now you're Jordan's mommy.
You store five sizes of clothes in your closet.
You call your husband on his cell phone in order to have a real conversation with him.
You go to bed at 12:30 A.M. and get up at 5:00 A.M., thankful for the extra sleep.
Excitement means Pampers are on sale.
You consider PBJs and Cheetos a nutritious meal.

You can change from lounging-sweats casual to night-on-the-town glamorous in three-and-a-half minutes.

"Doing lunch" means meeting three friends and their preschoolers at the McDonald's Playplace.

Hearing the words, "I'm done," from the bathroom sends chills up your spine.

You own more Disney movies than pairs of shoes.

You can pee with three children watching you—and only two are yours.

You spend more on babysitters than you do on utilities.

If you were trapped for days in your car, you could survive on the Cheerios and french fries on your floorboards.

You can tell what your daughter ate for breakfast, lunch and dinner by looking at the front of her T-shirt.

You willingly hug and kiss a kid who has sticky fingers, sweat-drenched hair and a milk mustache.

You're overworked, overcommitted and underappreciated—and you wouldn't trade your life for anything in the world.

Leslie Wilson

Bedtime Miracle

Between the dark and daylight, When the night is beginning to lower, Comes a pause in the day's occupation, That is known as the Children's Hour.
Henry Wadsworth Longfellow

I expected three small angels.
Instead, I got three kids,
All flesh-and-blood, three wiggleworms
Too quick to blow their lids.

I asked for little cherubs,
All sweet and pure and wise.
Instead, there's mischief, giggles, tears—
Each day some new surprise!

But at night when it is bedtime
And I kiss each shining face,
I find—oh, blessed miracle!—
Three angels in their place!

Bonnie Compton Hanson

Flannel in the Food Court

Sometimes it's hard to avoid the happiness of others.

David Assael

The smell of a wet golden retriever filled the bedroom, confirming that the tap-tippety-tap against my window was September rain. I burrowed deeper beneath the creamy comforter in hopes of delaying the usual morning chaos. While my husband hustled to get ready for work, I milked every mommy-minute—until there it was, the sound of mousy footsteps trickling down the hallway.

A tiny voice filled with naïve anticipation sang, "Good morning, Mommy! Is it Pajama Day?" And with that, the day had begun.

"Yes, it is!" I pulled back the covers and lifted Hayley into the warm bed. She held my face in her hands, rubbed noses and placed a big, wet kiss on my lips. I drank in the sweet, salty smell of her morning breath.

Fridays are the best days of the week. Fridays are Pajama Days.

They were birthed from an overflowing laundry basket

one cold, crummy morning. I'd made the desperate decision to rewash an entire load of laundry that had sat
unfolded in the basket for several days. It seemed less
daunting than ironing the wrinkled wardrobe. Unfortunately, several other loads of laundry waited
patiently for a spin, and we had few clean choices. So pajamas made the cut for the day's outfit.

By lunchtime my daughter asked the obvious, "When
do we get dressed?"

I stumbled for just a moment, and then these words
spilled out: "Didn't you know? Fridays are Pajama Days.
We get to stay in them all day long!"

Pajama Days became a sacred tradition.

Here we were, a year later, a perfect Friday morning.
Grand gray clouds hovered outside, bordering a dense
black sky. The rain was light, but persistent. I envisioned
cookie baking and finger painting.

"What would you like to do today?" I asked absently.

"Today we'll make teddy bears. You promised we'd
make bears, and today is the day."

Suddenly, the rain outside sounded ominous. My head
started to ache as I quickly searched through my mental
filing system. There it was, "The Promise." I had indeed
said we would make bears this week at a nearby mall. A
toy store there lets you make stuffed animals—pick out
the style, stuff, sew and clothe them. Fun possibilities,
but—today?

I'm not sure if it was the multitude of kisses covering
my face or the big, pleading eyes, but I quickly caved.
"Well, let's get ready quickly, and we can have breakfast at
the food court. Okay?" There was no resistance.

Hayley went one way, and I went the other. We were
making good time until I walked into the family
room. There she stood in her purple, fleecy-footed pajamas, neon-pink robe with its embroidered butterfly,

sunglasses, purse and a book fittingly titled *Pajama Time* by Sandra Boynton. My daughter took a good look at me and shunned the shades, asking, "Where are your pajamas, Mommy?" Her voice wavered just a little. "It is Pajama Day, right?"

"Yes, but we aren't going to stay home, so we need to put on some clothes," I answered.

The perfected pouter wound herself up and whined, "Pajamas are clothes." Tears welled up in her eyes.

A knot bunched in my stomach, rolling around and around and pushing its way up my throat, making me want to cry or yell. This day wasn't turning out the way I anticipated. She was going to ruin my Pajama Day.

I closed my eyes for a second before I addressed the inevitable temper tantrum, reminding myself that she was just three and this was her day, too. "You're right."

As we walked from our car to the mall entrance, I looked to see if anyone was watching. The drops had subsided, but I could still taste the rain, each breath mixed with a little pride and vanity. I'd made a grand attempt to disguise my outfit with glamorous hair and make-up. But there was no mistaking my gray and red plaid flannels for anything other than pajamas. And my tired cranberry robe was a poor imitation of a coat.

The mall was quiet. *This isn't so bad,* I thought. *No one is even here yet.* The fountains weren't on yet, and the shops were still dark inside. I started to relax.

But at the food court, I gasped to see the long line to the coffee stand. What in the world were these people going to think? What kind of mom lets her child go to the mall in nightwear? And what kind of woman dons the same?

The swish-swish of Hayley's footed pajamas shuffled on the mall floor and echoed down the hall. There was no turning back now.

Eyes peered curiously at the two of us as we stood in

line for our hot chocolate and muffins. Here I cowered in flannel PJs, all for the sake of keeping sacred our Pajama Day tradition. I'd obviously lost control to a preschooler.

A businessman behind us started to chat with Hayley. Before he asked the obvious, she brilliantly announced to him (and several onlookers), "Today is Pajama Day! On Fridays we wear pajamas all day!"

"Those are the best kinds of days to have." He winked at her. "I wish I could've worn pajamas instead of this suit."

"I'm sorry." Hayley nodded in sympathy. She reached out to pat the man's hand. "I guess not everyone has a mom like mine."

I stood a little straighter. It was the best Pajama Day ever.

Emily Okaty Wilson

Promises, Promises

Nobody can do for little children what grand-parents do. Grandparents sort of sprinkle stardust over the lives of little children.

Alex Haley

The summer my grandson was four, he stayed with us for a week. When it came time to take him home, I said, "Now, Victor, don't you go home and give away all your hugs and kisses. Be sure and save me some for next time you visit, okay?"

He wrapped his sweet little arms around my neck. "I won't, Grandma. I promise to save them for you."

A couple of weeks later, my daughter called. "Mom, would you please tell Victor that it's okay for him to give me kisses and hugs?"

"What?"

"At bedtime, no hugs or kisses. In the morning, no kisses and hugs. None for hellos, none for good-byes." Vina worked herself into a huff. "Victor simply refuses. And I put the blame squarely on *you*."

"Why? What does Victor say?" My shoulders shook with suppressed laughter.

"'I promised Grandma,' he says. So, *Grandma*, can you tell me what's up?"

"Vina, I can't imagine what this has to do with me. I certainly didn't tell him not to . . ." I suddenly recalled—and recounted—our conversation upon his departure.

"You told him to save all his hugs and kisses for you . . . and he took it seriously!" Now I could hear a bit of a smile in her voice. "Would you please release him from his promise?"

I thought a moment. "Put Victor on the phone."

"Hello, Grandma."

"Hello, sweetheart. Have you been saving all your hugs and kisses for me?"

"Uh huh, just like I promised."

"Well, I can't wait until I see you. So, can you give them all to me right now?"

"Okay, Grandma." And into the telephone, Victor released precious little smacks and big umm-umm-umms.

"There, that's all, Grandma."

I replied, "Now, will you do Grandma a big favor?"

"Okay."

"Go give your mother lots of hugs and kisses—from me to her."

Victor dropped the phone with a thud and began his favor for Grandma.

I could hear lots of smacking, several umm-umm-umms . . . and Vina's laughter. And, just before I hung up, I heard my daughter shout from a distance, "Forever and ever, Mom!"

Christine M. Smith

In His Second Year

Who is getting more pleasure from this rocking, the baby or me?

Nancy Thayer

I love the time when he first wakes
From his afternoon nap.
I listen for the pad of his bare feet in the hall.
He stands there, silently gazing at me, yawning
And rubbing his eyes with his fists.
I gather him up,
Still soft and rosy with sleep.
He curls in my lap,
His head against me, his eyes half open,
And together we silently rock.
He is so gentle, so little
And so very vulnerable.
I hold him and love him selfishly;
He is my baby again
For these few short minutes.
Then slowly his drowsiness dissolves.
He wiggles and squirms to get away

And explore this all-too-exciting world.
I can hold him no longer.
He struggles down and runs laughing from me.
I return to the kitchen,
But I am content.
For a fleeting, too-brief moment,
I had captured a butterfly in its flight.

Michele Ivy Davis
As appreared in Home Life Magazine

Without Words

Love is everything it's cracked up to be . . . it really is worth fighting for, being brave for, risking everything for.

Erica Jong

We flew halfway around the world to adopt a child.

Leaving behind winter-wet Oregon and three sons, we landed in the bitterly cold Ukraine, eager to meet our new toddler.

Our teen daughter accompanied us to the adoption center in Kiev where we viewed files. But it was the folder on almost-three Vladamir that caught our eye. We knew he belonged to us.

Escorted by a hired driver, we left during the night on a six-hour trip to Kharkiv along pot-holed roads in a swirling snowstorm. The director, who spoke only Russian, greeted us warmly at the orphanage. A translator prepared us to meet Vladamir, whom they called Vova.

Then in he walked, a little brunette boy. Handsome and busy, he soon captured our hearts. He touched everything in the director's office, her telephone, her television and items on her desk. When we gave him a little red match-box car, he gripped it with delight.

The director invited us to watch a performance in the music class down the hall. As the piano played and the children sang a song, Vova rode around the room on a stick horse, fell over and was rescued by two girls. Language wasn't a barrier; we understood the plot and fell in love with the hero.

During the week the paperwork was being completed, we visited Vova twice a day. We pointed at objects in books and told him the English words. We showed him pictures of his new brothers, sister, dog and cat, and our home in Oregon. We played soccer together. Fun was a language we all spoke.

Although Vova was quiet, solemn and rarely smiled, we sensed his tender spirit. Concerned, however, we asked if he ever spoke. But our cares evaporated the day we gave him a toy cell phone we purchased at an outdoor market. He chattered to the other little orphans, bragging that his new mama and papa had given it to him. We understood his excitement. It felt the same in Russian as English.

At the court hearing, Vova officially became our son. We renamed him Luke and rode the train to Kiev. The officials complimented his ready acceptance of this American family he barely knew and couldn't really communicate with.

We arrived at our flat late that night. Luke nestled in the middle of the bed between my husband and I, snuggling a small, stuffed toy. We clicked off the lights, and our sweet son went right to sleep. American and Ukrainian—we were all weary.

In the morning, I woke first and just looked at the precious boy lying next to me. Would he be startled to wake next to virtual strangers? I watched his eyes flutter then shut. He turned his head toward me and opened them again. When he jumped in surprise, I murmured reassurances and handed him our travel alarm clock to play with. He seemed to understand and immediately calmed.

After a bit, he stood on the bed and peered out the window at the busy street and sidewalks seven floors below. Excited, Luke jabbered about "machinas." Obviously, he liked cars most of all. A mother can tell these things, no matter the language.

Later, he pointed to himself and said, "Luke"—one of his first words in English.

I pulled him into my arms. Luke was our new son, the answer to our prayers. And I knew the love we'd feel for each other would need no translation. Love, you see, transcends all barriers.

Diane Kagey

Career-Minded

The wisest men follow their own direction.

Euripides

His given name is John, but we call him Jack after his great-grandfather, this miracle baby who blesses our family.

From the moment I first held him in my arms, I recognized his gentle nature, easy-going personality and sensitive spirit. I pondered who and what he might someday become and—on the spot—I began to spin and weave my dreams.

Jack loves music, so every night I sing a hymn to him as he melds his head into my neck. And when we play his favorite Jana Alayra video, he and Madison "jump to the light, light, light" while he imitates his sister's hand motions.

He's got rhythm, I think. *I bet he'll lead the church choir. On a crusade. Worldwide.*

When it's time for our nightly prayers, Jack darts straight to the bedroom. He kneels, folds his hands and closes his eyes without any prompting from us.

He's spiritual, I glow with satisfaction. *He'll be a man of the cloth, a beloved pastor someday. I wouldn't mind that a bit.*

Yet, Jack is all b-o-y—with a capital "B." He climbs everything in sight. *An admired mountaineer,* I decide. As he *vroom-vrooms* his toy trucks across my floors, I reconsider. *An innovative automotive engineer?*

He spends hours in the kitchen, opening and closing the cupboard doors. *Hmmm,* I dream on, *a designer? No, an architect, I bet.* I nod decisively. *This kid is definitely destined to be and do great things!*

Actually—I come to realize—he's obsessed with doors, and not just those in the kitchen. All doors. The front door, the back door, the bathroom door. The French doors, doggie doors, playhouse doors. Open and close, open and close, open and . . . it's enough to drive a less career-oriented mommy nuts.

Which brings me to this evening. Here we are dining at our favorite Italian eatery—kid-friendly, with paper and crayons to occupy our little ones. But Jack, to my surprise, doesn't show an artistic bent. Instead, he bounces toward the restaurant's front door.

"Honey," I follow him, "get out of the way. People are coming in and out."

Jack isn't listening. He's too busy . . . opening the door and stepping to the side as a couple enters.

"Thank you, young man," they say, smiling at my preschooler.

Encouraged, Jack holds the door as a woman walks through. "What a nice little gentleman," she praises my son.

He pushes it wide to accommodate a family of teenagers. "Hey, there, buddy. Thanks for muscling the door."

Jack beams, obviously hooked and happy in his new-found career.

I smile inwardly—more at myself than my son. *I guess Jack has a mind of his own.* And I nod my head in acceptance. *My son . . . the doorman!*

Maria Nickless

Purple Principles

Imagination continually frustrates tradition; that is its function.

John Pfeiffer

"Mom?"

That nap hadn't lasted long, I sighed. I glanced from the newspaper as my four-year-old entered the room.

"What is it, Puss?"

"Can I have my toenails painted today?"

Asleep one minute and toenails the next; I blinked. What went on inside that head? I was constantly amazed by this little pinball-machine mind.

"Er, why do you want your toenails painted?"

"Because Ben and Ollie had red toenails yesterday, and it looked so good."

I considered that for a moment. Was he talking about the O'Neill twins? "Ben and Ollie are boys, right?"

A puzzled nod and a raised eyebrow told me I'd asked a dumb question. "Who painted the twins' toenails?"

"Their mom, of course."

"So," I inquired, casually, "do the boys have their toenails painted often?"

"Yes, and now I want you to do mine. I want red toes, too."

I stared at his pleased little face and shifted uncomfortably on the stool. I considered saying I'd run out of nail polish—much easier than explaining that boys don't usually wear nail polish. But I wasn't up for an endless round of the *why* questions it would evoke.

"Do you know something else, Mom?" He pulled off his socks and tweaked his toes at me. "Sometimes Ben and Ollie's mom even paints each toe a different color."

I looked at him cross-legged on the rug, eyes wide with admiration for someone else's mom, and instantly I reached a decision.

"Right, Paddy!" I swooped him off the floor. "Let's see what we've got in the bathroom."

"No red, only purple."

"I love purple," he whooped.

"Me, too," I whooped right back.

We painted our toenails in a sweet mother-and-son moment. I thought about Ben and Ollie's mom—with whom I vaguely remembered exchanging a hurried greeting or two as we flew in and out of the preschool Paddy attended four days a week since I'd returned to work. His grandparents kept him on Fridays.

I imagined her as a strong cookie-figure, regularly painting her sons' toenails, thumbing her nose at gender stereotypes and flying in the face of convention. I, too, could be that sort of mother; I decorated Paddy's toenails with flourish, vowing to tune in to all reports of Ben and Oliver O'Neill from now on.

But my newfound confidence took its first jolt about an hour later when my husband returned from work and Paddy gleefully told him how we'd spent our time.

"Well, that's great," I heard him say in a curious, strangled voice. He took the stairs in twos to reach me. "Why did you paint his nails?" he mouthed urgently, eyes wide in horror.

"Oh, relax, Pete. Ben and Oliver O'Neill have their toe-nails colored, too," I reassured. He seemed a little mollified but looked askance at the offending nails for the rest of the week.

And he wasn't the only one. Living on the other side of the world did not stop my Scottish mother from voicing her opinion in the toenail debate two days later.

"Gran wants to speak to you." Paddy relinquished the phone after thirty minutes, during which time the subject of toenails had evidently been discussed.

"What are you doing painting that boy's toes?" she asked. "It's terrible! You'll turn him into a girl."

My father-in-law apparently felt the same way. At the end of the week, I picked up Paddy from his Friday stay with Pete's parents.

"Grandad says I'm a sissle," Paddy informed me as we got into the car.

"A what?"

"A sissle. And I don't want to be a sissle, Mom." His voice was forlorn. "We'll have to take off my nail polish when we get home."

"Why?" I was baffled.

"Only a sissle wears nail polish," he said, sounding remarkably like his grandfather.

"Oh, you mean a *sissy*," I corrected him.

He nodded sadly.

"What do you think that word means?"

"It means you're a big *girl*."

"So, is Mommy a sissle . . . I mean a sissy, then?"

"No, Mommy," he almost smiled. "Only boys can be sissles. Grandad said."

Bloody Grandad.

"But what about Ben and Ollie?"

"Grandad says they're sissles, too."

In a fleeting moment, I saw him step back from his magical world of innocence and make-believe, of dress-ups and suspended reality, and I knew that something precious was about to be lost.

Not today, though. Not if I could help it. I resorted to guerrilla tactics.

"Well, that's a shame," I said carefully. "I liked your purple toenails and, you know, there's nothing wrong with being a sissle. Sometimes Grandad is one, too." Through my rearview mirror, I watched his eyes widen.

"When?" he asked, still unconvinced.

I thought about the photograph of my husband's father taken by me two years ago. He'd played the part of Juliet in his local theatrical production of "Romeo and Juliet—with a Twist." Posing for my camera had been the least he could do after I'd just sat through that painful debacle.

No nail polish, but plenty of purple tulle. Nice one, Grandad.

"Well, Paddy," I began, "I've got this photograph. . . ."

Somehow, I was betting the purple toes would survive to fight another day.

Maureen Johnson

The House That Mommy Built

Our children give us the opportunity to become the parent we always wished we'd had.

Louise Hart

Our cramped apartment often triggered tempers, and sometimes even two-year-old Mike knew he needed a time-out. But, where? There was no place to go, no place for him to be quiet and safe by himself.

After one particularly difficult session of his strong will pitted against mine, I decided we needed to go for a walk to soothe our jangled nerves. His *and* mine.

I bundled him and put a thin coating of Vaseline over his rosy cheeks to protect him from the single-digit temperature. And then I stuffed him into the carrier on my back, snug against the cold. With a handful of letters for the post office and some wrapped homemade cookies, we were off.

We took the long way through the neighborhood so we could stop at the pet store. "Whatcha wanna see today, Mike?" The proprietor greeted us. "Let's see. How about . . ." He held a wiggling lizard out for Mike to meet. "Sorta looks like a miniature dinosaur, don't he?"

I offered the shopkeeper cookies as I did almost every time we visited.

"You don't have to do that—just keep bringin' the little fella by."

After lingering farewells to all of Mike's pet-shop favorites, we headed to the post office. In the alley I saw something that gave me an idea, and we ducked into the appliance store next door. The stock boy didn't know what to make of my request but gamely gave me permission to take anything I wanted.

Moments later we were on our way home, with Mike riding on my back, craning his neck to watch the refrigerator box bumping behind us—plowing over shrubs, small dogs and anyone else who happened to be in the way.

Mike's squeals of delight warned passersby as he pointed and called out, "Mommy-box! Mommy-box!"

Every block or so, I adjusted my numb grip on the tattered flap. I lost my balance several times, but we arrived home, the bedraggled box—and us—still in one piece. Mike now slumped deep in the backpack, fast asleep.

After tucking him into his bed, I set to work. Time flew as I sliced, squiggled designs and fashioned furniture out of small boxes and an old, overturned laundry basket. Eventually I heard a giggle behind me. I moved aside, and the sight that greeted Mike lit up his little face like a Christmas tree.

"House!" He jumped up and down, then ran through the door I'd cut in the box and immediately crawled inside. He beamed, "Me house!"

The refrigerator box-turned-clubhouse became his favorite haunt. When he was tired or grumpy, I suggested he take a "time-out" in his house. Many times I found him asleep surrounded by trucks and dolls. Eventually, he dragged his books in there, too. I heard him read to imaginary friends, tapping the pictures and telling the story his way: "Mommy took me on a walk and we found my box. . . ."

Maryjo Faith Morgan

Hair Today

Like so many things one did for children, it was absurd but pleasing, and the pleasure came from the anticipation of their pleasure.

Mary Gordon

"I have something to tell you," my husband wakes me in a gentle voice. "You have to promise not to yell." My eyes flew open. "And you can't cry, either."

I got dressed and followed him upstairs. Like a scene from a bad movie, he inched open our daughter's bedroom door.

"What happened?" I screeched.

No one answered.

"What happened here?" I demanded.

"Well, I thought she was with me, but she wasn't," my husband stumbled over his words, "and then I saw her in the bathroom, and she looked like this."

"Look, Mommy, Emily has pretty hair," my almost-four-year-old bragged.

All I could do was wail.

Her hair—her beautiful, shoulder-length hair. Gone. At

least, the *top* was gone. Emily had created an inverted Mohawk, snipping away a four-inch swath across her head. And it looked terrible. So terrible that there was only one solution.

I pouted as I watched my sister-in-law shave Emily bald.

Preschool, I moaned. *Think of the teasing she'll get.*

But, gaining my composure, I commented, "Oh, Emily, this will be so nice and cool for summer." Yet each time I glanced at her, my heart sank.

Emily became self-conscious.

"Mommy, am I still a girl?" she questioned.

"Mommy, am I still pretty?" she wavered.

So to make her feel better, I did what any insane mother would do: I cut off my hair, too. Emily was thrilled. Now she and Mommy looked alike. She stopped doubting her beauty and now declared how pretty she and Mommy were.

When I saw her newfound joy, I reconsidered this whole hair thing. It is, after all, just hair. It will grow back. It isn't who I am or who she is. I also learned the "lengths" I'll go to ensure my daughter's happiness.

Besides, short hair really is much cooler in the summer.

Amanda L. Stevens

Mothering: The Next Generation

The most important thing she'd learned over the years was that there was no way to be a perfect mother and a million ways to be a good one.

Jill Churchill

Of all the astonishments of motherhood, watching my own daughters become mothers tops the list. Of all the rewards I could have asked for in life, this is the sweetest.

My daughters are better at motherhood than I ever was. And that's not just false modesty, believe me. They were better prepared. They were not just smarter; they were wiser, too. And they were surely more ready to accept all the colossal challenges than I was when I became a mother at twenty-one.

These same daughters who once drove me crazy, who left their rooms in post-hurricane condition, who failed to send thank-you notes to their relatives for decades, have found their calling.

I watched Jill, Amy and Nancy swell with pregnancies and become responsible, conscientious mothers-to-be, reading voraciously and knowing what every single week of development meant. I spent those same months flying blind, more child than woman and surely not ready for the enormous job ahead.

I'm ashamed to admit that I ate carelessly, didn't exercise and never even considered breastfeeding back in the early 1960s when having babies, for most women, was an automatic-pilot experience. "Don't ask, don't tell" might have been our motto before a new generation began to question and learn and reshape not just their bodies, but the entire pregnancy experiences.

But I was still a bit stunned when the daughters—who never took their vitamins, seldom ate right and got no sleep for years on end during college—were unrelentingly vigilant about their health the moment they became pregnant. I almost couldn't believe what I was seeing and hearing.

Natural childbirth? A given. Ditto for nursing. Jill, Amy and Nancy were absolutely committed to doing everything right.

Yet when the babies came, our daughters greeted them with the same awe, wonderment and surrender that women have for centuries. They were as overwhelmed as we all are when a tiny, helpless infant is placed in our arms—and in our perpetual care.

Jill, the oldest, became a mother first. The birth turned our daughter, the hard-bitten public defender, into a marshmallow. Her sisters were no less vulnerable.

"Hello, my daughter," Amy said through persistent tears when she greeted her first baby. Forget the corporate world, high-powered meetings and Manhattan art galleries. Amy's new master was a tiny tyrant with an impressive set of lungs.

A second daughter arrived, and Amy continued the ultimate tightrope walk: balancing love and work, home and job.

And Nancy, the daughter who yearned so for a daughter, has instead greeted three sons. And she's fallen madly, hopelessly in love with the bruisers.

In so many ways, each of our daughters has shown a new and unexpected side of herself. So in joyously welcoming our grandchildren, I have also re-met their mothers—my daughters. I have witnessed their strength and courage, stamina and commitment, self-sacrifice and energy.

My daughters are mothers—fine, loving, generous ones. Better ones than I could have imagined. And what a sweet, sweet reward that is for any mother—emeritus.

Sally Friedman

$\overline{3}$

INSIGHTS
AND LESSONS

*As we get older it seems we lose faith in our
ability to express ourselves as purely. Little
children have a way of reminding us of our
original purpose: joy.*

Marie Osmond

Food for Thought

Parents learn a lot from their children about coping with life.

Muriel Spark

When you're the mother of a small boy, even mundane activities like grocery shopping can take unexpected turns—as I learned one Sunday afternoon.

Griffin and I browsed the bread aisle when a grandmotherly-looking woman paused near us. "Are you helping Mommy with the shopping?" she asked.

My son ducked behind me with the classic shyness of a four-year-old. The woman and I exchanged smiles.

As she moved down the aisle, Griffin peered around me to say in a loud voice, "She's really old, isn't she?"

"Shh!" I winced.

When the woman turned back to look at us, I apologized. She merely laughed. "That's okay. He's right."

When she left, I turned to Griffin. "Honey, it's not nice to say somebody's old."

"Why not? It's true."

I'd taught Griffin the importance of telling the truth

rather than fabricating stories to get out of trouble. Now I had to explain the subtle distinction between honesty and courtesy. "Just because something's true doesn't mean it's nice. People don't always like being reminded that they're getting older. It can hurt their feelings."

"Why?"

"It's just not a good idea to talk about how old people are. If you have something to say about how a person looks, please don't say it where they can hear you. Save it to tell me later."

The next Saturday, my boss, Paul, phoned and asked me to take care of a small emergency project. My husband was away for the day, and I had no one to watch Griffin.

"Bring him with you," Paul said. "The job will take only an hour. I'll entertain him."

When we arrived, Paul had markers and paper for Griffin. From my cubicle, I could hear them chatting about Griffin's drawings.

Then my candid son asked, "What happened to your hair?"

Dead silence followed.

Paul, a handsome man of forty, was prematurely balding. "It just kind of fell out," he finally answered.

"You should buy some new hair," Griffin suggested.

I cringed. The kindest thing I could do was pretend I hadn't heard. I finished my work, and we left.

"Paul can't help that his hair's falling out," I told Griffin on the way home. "Remember me saying it's not nice to talk about how people look? We need to try not to hurt people's feelings."

"Okay, Mommy," Griffin said.

But I knew he was merely expressing his observations. How could he possibly understand that baldness, like age, might be a sensitive subject?

The following Saturday, we pulled into a fast-food

drive-through. A teenage girl in the pick-up window handed me a milkshake.

"I ordered chocolate, not strawberry." I handed it back.

She returned with another milkshake and a bag containing a cherry pie and french fries.

"I ordered a burger and a child's meal," I pointed out.

Griffin's voice rang, loud and clear, from the backseat. "Boy, she isn't very good at her job, is she?"

"Griffin, shhh!" I wished I could disappear.

The girl handed me another bag without a word.

"I'm sorry," I said. She didn't answer, so I drove away.

"Honey, you shouldn't have said that. You hurt that girl's feelings. I know it seems like she isn't very good at her job, but everybody makes mistakes. Maybe she's having a tough day."

"I'm sorry, Mommy," Griffin said.

I sighed. "It's okay. Just try not to do it again."

The next day was Sunday, grocery-shopping day. Thinking of Griffin's recent social blunders, I suggested he stay home with his dad.

He burst into tears. "I promise I'll be good!"

I knew I couldn't leave the child at home forever, fearing he'd say something hurtful or embarrassing. "Okay," I sighed, "but don't say anything about how people look or how they do their job!"

At the grocery deli, we took a number and waited our turn among the line of customers. A store employee pushed a cart containing samples of yellow cake. "Would you like to try some pound cake?" she asked. "I can give you a dollar-off coupon."

"No, thank you," I said.

"No, thank you," Griffin echoed.

I held my breath as the woman moved away to offer cake to other customers, all of whom also declined. She was white-haired and stooped, but—to my relief—Griffin didn't mention her age.

After we made our deli selections, we headed to frozen foods.

"Mommy, remember that lady with the cake?"

"Yes." I dropped a bag of frozen broccoli in our cart. Now he'd probably tell me she was really old. At least he'd waited until she was out of earshot.

"Nobody wanted her cake," he said.

"Maybe they don't like pound cake."

"But how do you think that made her feel?"

I caught my breath. "I don't know. How do you think it made her feel?"

"Sad."

I hadn't given a thought to the woman's feelings. The store surely paid her wages whether or not anyone tried the cake. Still, I imagined how she might feel, offering samples to people more interested in watching for their deli number than sampling her cake. Some customers hadn't even glanced at her when they declined.

But the real point was that my four-year-old son had not only absorbed all my lectures on others' feelings, but had taken the lessons to a level I hadn't even considered.

I hugged him. "You're so nice, Griffin. Should we go tell her we'd like to try some cake?"

He nodded, and I grabbed a pound cake from the freezer. We would ask the woman for a coupon, too. Humbled, I followed my son—who might have a four-year-old's brutal honesty, but could teach his mother about compassion.

Lisa Wood Curry

On the Table

The people who make a difference are not the ones with the credentials, but the ones with the concern.

Max Lucado

When our oldest child was just over a year old, my husband and I treated ourselves to our very first, brand-new, bought-because-we-loved-it piece of furniture. Like many young families, we lived with hand-me-downs and garage sale finds. In fact, we'd told the saleswoman we were "just looking," and it was true—until we spotted it: the perfect coffee table.

Made of two-by-fours, the pine box weighed a ton. I was initially drawn to it because of the storage space inside. Space my year-old son couldn't get at. Space to store my magazines so they wouldn't get wrinkled or shredded or . . . chewed. Space for knickknacks that couldn't stand up to the curious manipulations of a child who didn't take "no" seriously.

I especially loved the lid. When opened, its surface remained horizontal—thanks to oddly convoluted arm hinges—and was the perfect height for dining when we sat on the couch. I envisioned romantic dinners after the baby was bedded down for the night.

I decided the coffee table would be the first piece in a room full of matching furniture. I pictured it in my mind: stylish, comfortable, a room for adults. A room where I could put things the way I wanted them . . . and they'd stay that way.

To save money, we purchased the unfinished version. After hours of sanding, staining, hand waxing and polishing, we were rewarded with a golden-hued, satin-smooth table. The magnificent focal point of our family room.

Because of the table's pristine beauty, I made rules. Drinks must be on coasters. Feet were forbidden to rest upon it. Toys were not allowed to touch it.

These rules lasted for, oh, about a week. Until our son adopted the table as his hand rail so he could practice his walking skills. I bent the rules; a few fingerprints were worth the minutes of amusement this activity gave him.

But the day he stumbled and hit the corner of the table with his front teeth was the day everything changed. Fortunately, the baby was unscathed. Not so the table.

Two tiny teeth imprints marred its surface. My unblemished table was no more. Its golden-hued, satin-smooth finish was ruined. The dream of my perfect "someday" room was destroyed.

But the more I looked at the table, the more his cute imprints grew on me. We pointed them out to everyone who visited as a kind of conversation piece. And they did not exist alone for long.

Today, I can see where wooden toy trains derailed and crashed . . . again and again and again. Where T. rex went on tirades, and block towers teetered and fell. Where budding artists practiced their skills.

The table has endured feet (in and out of socks) and

survived sippy-cup leaks and teething drool. It's been the base for a dollhouse's backyard, the checkout counter for a grocery store and the backdrop for teddy bear teas. It's witnessed round after round of Dino Bingo and Go Fish.

My husband and I have only actually used it for romantic dinners twice, and, I must confess, the coffee table now doubles as my workout bench.

Its once pristine surface is pitted, pocked ... and perfect. It's our family's story, past, present and future. An heirloom-in-the-making. A real conversation piece.

Lizann Flatt

Blown Away

Children have never been very good at listening to their elders, but they have never failed to imitate them.

James Baldwin

It's really true that we have to teach through behavior, not just with words.

I used to chide my three-year-old son, Noah, "You must learn to be patient" or "You have got to learn to wait," all the while knowing that patience is not one of my finer qualities. In fact, I'm terribly impatient. I've always recognized this and tried to catch myself before I blew my top in front of him, but it wasn't until he started calling other drivers "idiot" that I knew I had to change.

In an effort to control my impatience, I gritted my teeth and forced myself to wait. But my body language spoke as loudly as my words. My jaw clenched; my shoulders rose up; my arms and legs stiffened. Had steam come out of my ears, I could have been a cartoon character.

Noah saw it all. That was no better.

I tried weighing the importance of each situation.

Sometimes I was able to calm myself down, but I have a very fine point of focus. Too often even the little things seemed important at that moment. Why was the ring on the milk jug so hard to get off? Who left the bathroom light on again? Where did all the pens go? These little things undermined my sense of control. So much of my life involved managing details, and I wasn't used to relinquishing the reins. I needed to broaden my scope.

So I focused on the "big picture" whenever possible. I counted my blessings—my family, home, dishwasher and flush toilets. Sometimes it worked, but I didn't always remember the larger meanings of the journey of life while in line at the grocery store. It was the store's fault for not having enough checkouts open. It was other people's fault for needing so much food. It was the clock's fault for ticking so fast.

These absurd thoughts raced through my head like a bad habit. It crushed me to realize I was transferring this negativism and criticism to Noah. I just couldn't find a way to stop myself.

Then one morning, Noah was engrossed in peeling the price tag off a book while I struggled to get him dressed. We weren't in our usual rush, but I could feel my blood rising. I felt frustrated, and then I felt frustrated at *feeling* frustrated.

Exasperated, I sat down and looked at my son. "I'm sorry, Noah. I'm no good at this. I think you should teach me how to be patient."

"It's easy, Mama," he said. "Sometimes at school we want to go outside, and we say, 'Mrs. B, when are we going outside? When are we going outside?' and she says, 'Oh, you kids. We have music or snack first, and you have to *be patient*. Just put it in your hands and blow it away like this.'"

Noah cupped his hands in front of his face, puffed up

his cheeks and blew. "And that's patience, see Mama? You just blow it!"

As I watched him demonstrate, my frustration dissolved into laughter.

I don't know if he realized that it was the laughter that calmed me down, but from then on, whenever I got impatient and Noah was nearby, he'd say, "Be patient, Mama. Just blow it!" I'd laugh again and mock blowing out a big breath into my hands.

Yes, I've always known that example is the best way to learn. I just never expected that my child would be the teacher and I would be the student.

Kristin Walker

The Potty Predicament

Whoever is out of patience is out of possession of his soul.

Sir Francis Bacon

I bought a potty seat for my son before he turned a year old, a colorful, deluxe model with removable parts, front-loading plastic bowl and sure-grip sides. I'd had glorious visions, almost since I left the delivery room, of my brilliant progeny fully trained and diaper-free by eighteen months. Heck, make that fifteen months.

We'd be the envy of all my friends, whose deficient toddlers remained untrained at age two.

I kept the commode in the closet for a few weeks, not wanting to place unrealistic expectations on my son. When I finally placed it, with much fanfare, in the bathroom, the child seemed delighted. He examined it closely, giggled and squealed while I beamed as I planned how to spend the money I'd save on diapers.

Over the next few months, however, the potty was transformed into a nagging symbol of intergenerational warfare. The first skirmish—over positioning—raged throughout the house and left me exhausted and demoralized. I would place the potty in the bathroom, only to return a few hours, minutes or even seconds later to find it missing. Various "removable parts" would appear in closets, under my bed, in my husband's underwear drawer, in the sandbox—even floating in the birdbath.

The bowl—the heart of the contraption—was chewed and colored on and used as a collection bin for toys, books and even feminine hygiene products unthinkingly left within reach.

Something about the seat aroused my son's creative energies. It elicited intricate crayon drawings and doubled as a playpen for his stuffed animals. As his strength, coordination and evil intent grew, the fruit-of-my-womb figured out how to fill the bowl from the bathtub and drained it in a trail across the carpet.

I launched a new campaign.

Every hour on the hour, I dragged my son, kicking and screaming, into the bathroom. I'd read his favorite stories in animated voices. I sang his favorite song, "John Jacob Jingleheimer Schmidt." No luck.

Thinking a target might help, I floated Cheerios in water to challenge his competitive instincts. He scooped up the soggy circles and crammed them in his mouth. I invoked the dreadful specter of peer pressure. "Do you want to be the only two-year-old still in diapers?" While I nearly wept at the prospect, my son was impervious to public opinion.

His second birthday came and went, and I lost sleep, picturing him at high-school graduation in Huggies— Extra, Extra Large.

Desperate, I played my trump card—bribery—promising him candy for each success. His eyes gleamed in sweet anticipation, but still, the kid wouldn't give in. Frustrated beyond words, I resorted to coercion, holding him, squirming furiously, on the potty. I did it only once. He deliberately baptized me in righteous indignation.

As the three-year mark approached, he was upstaged by younger children who pranced proudly to the potty. Despondent at my failure, I deployed a final weapon. I put away the potty and bought a large supply of Pull-Ups. When he informed me that he needed to be changed, I acted deliriously happy.

After all those agonizing months, this strategy succeeded in exactly two days. My demon seed started using the toilet as if he'd been doing it all his life. Now, more than a year later, I can't get him out of the bathroom. He has in-depth conversations with himself or an imaginary friend. Walking by the bathroom one day, I heard him say, "Would you like to see what a penis looks like?" Dazed, I continued down the hall, wondering what I'd created.

My daughter recently turned two. When I get out of therapy in another year or so, I might try to train her. Or maybe I'll just invest in Huggies—Extra, Extra Large.

Jackie Papandrew

"Why do I need to learn potty training? Is it something I'll use later in life? Will it help me get into a good college? Do chicks dig guys who are potty trained?"

The Green One

Being a mother, as far as I can tell, is a constantly evolving process of adapting to the needs of your child while also changing and growing as a person in your own right.

Deborah Insel

"I want the green one!" My nine-year-old shouted from the passenger seat beside me. His five-year-old sister burst into angry tears.

"No, I want the green one. You always get to pick first!"

From my vantage point in the driver's seat, I could see directly into the basket of lollipops being offered by the bank teller at the drive-through. *All* of the lollipops were green, a fact my son had noticed as the opportunity of a lifetime. By calling for the green one, he could amuse himself and unsettle his sister at the same time.

I sighed and accepted two green lollipops.

When had my role as mother deteriorated into referee? I'd somehow thought my kids would rise above the constant rivalry and bickering that defined my own childhood. I should have known better.

The first time Alison broke one of Mitch's toys, the lines were drawn and the battle waged. Until then, she had been *the baby*, a cute little thing who liked to cover his eyes with her chubby hands during his favorite cartoon show. Annoying but tolerable. Getting into his stuff and breaking things was another matter. Big brother declared war— a war that continued until he moved into his own apartment twenty years later.

Twenty years! I spent almost half of my life breaking up arguments and sending opponents to neutral corners. I once assumed I could avoid sibling rivalry by loving them equally. Ha! For twenty-two years, Christmas gifts were purchased according to evenly matched price tags, privileges doled out at identical ages and cake servings measured to the nth degree.

At times, I thought it would be easier to raise geraniums.

Mitch and Alison quarreled over television shows, telephone calls and whose turn it was to do the dishes. Most often they fought over nothing at all. You know—"She's bugging me," or "He's making a face at me again." It seemed they were unhappy to occupy the same house. Or planet.

No advice column or book offered a solution that worked in our home. I tried a variety of strategies and punishments, but nothing eliminated or even decreased the fighting. Time-outs provided opportunities for plotting revenge. Increased chore assignments caused disputes over who had the more difficult duties. My most frequent response—yelling—probably made the neighbors think I'd lost my marbles.

Or maybe they were too busy yelling at their own kids to notice.

So how did I cope with fighting children? I waited them out. I knew they'd grow up some day. They *had* to. I hoped they'd eventually put away their childish bickering and learn to like each other. Guess what? They did.

The year my daughter graduated from high school, she and her brother, her life-long enemy, took a trip to Disneyland together. He let her drive his new car; she helped with gas money. They had a blast.

Later, he recommended her for a job in his office, and they drove to work together. Five days a week, twenty-five minutes each way. In the same car, in heavy traffic. My son and my daughter—together. That was several years ago, and I still haven't gotten over it.

Yes, kids do grow up, mature even. The fighting ceases, and they start to love each other. Meanwhile, we moms must grit our teeth, pray for patience and wait. It worked for me, and I'll bet it will work for you, too.

But I still keep a supply of green lollipops on hand—just in case.

June Williams

Off the Mark, *by Mark Parisi. Reprinted by permission of Mark Parisi.*

Through the Looking Glass

*Becoming a mother doesn't mean abandoning
the girl you once were but rather embracing her
and introducing her to your children.*

Rachel Ryan

Every year we attend the county fair.

I can't wait for the aroma of funnel cakes to send me on
a kamikaze mission straight to the concession stand. My
children, on the other hand, can't wait to climb aboard
the death-wish rides and eat cotton candy. Sometimes
my funnel cakes and their rides don't sit well together,
but we still manage to have a great time.

This past year, Jessica and I visited the fun house. We
stumbled across the moving floor, giggled through the
laughing pen and arrived at the room of mirrors. There
were mirrors that made us short and chunky, tall and
skinny, and even one that made us look wavy.

Four-year-old Jessica loves looking at her reflection, but
at the wavy mirror she started to cry.

"What's wrong, sweetie?" I gave her a comforting hug.

"I look ugly, Mommy." She sobbed as she gazed at her

distorted self. "I want to be me again."

Resisting an urge to laugh, I urged her outside and opened my compact. "Those were trick mirrors," I explained. "Now look at yourself, Jessica. See how pretty you are? You're still the same little girl. We found her again." And I led her to a concession stand for a candy apple and a sensory break.

It wasn't until later that I applied the experience to my own life.

How often do I have a distorted perception of myself? So many days I wash dishes and laundry and kids, pick up the same toys one hundred times, and dine a la alphabet soup with ketchup and pea-stained preschoolers. Then I stare in the bathroom mirror, wondering at the self-pitying woman reflected back. Like Jessica, I, too, am scared at that ugly, warped version of me.

And I realize the image is merely clouded and "wavy" just like the mirror in the fun house. Certainly not a true reflection of the woman who also basks in the rays of her children's love and laughter.

And I give myself a break. I grab the children—and a box of Little Debbie cakes—and head outside to find my true self again.

Lisa Moffitt

The Critter Brigade

It's very important to give children a chance.

Nikki Giovanni

The Critter Brigade was out early this morning. Through the kitchen window I could see them: seven-year-old Haley, five-year-old Molly and three-year-old Hewson scrambling through the irises, still in their pajamas, soaked with dew and gaining on what looked like a tiny tree frog.

I was pulling for the frog, but the little fellow was too slow. The next I saw of him, he was peering out from Molly's fist with a look that seemed to say I was his only hope of seeing the outside world again. Haley trailed Molly with a hand full of leaves and grass. "Here, let's put him in a jar with these. We'll make it just like his house outside."

They scoured the cabinets for just the right container as I subtly dispensed my first dose of guilt. I've got this down to a science. "Ya'll didn't happen to see his mom or dad anywhere around, did you? I hope they're not getting worried about him."

But nobody was paying attention to me. They were too busy writing name suggestions on slips of paper and mixing them up in a bowl. "Mom, what would you like our frog's name to be?"

"Well . . . gee . . . I thought we might just keep him a few minutes then let him go. Don't you think he'd be happier in his own environment where everything's familiar?"

Hewson jumped up and down hollering, "Darth Vader! Darth Vader! His name is Darth Vader!"

"Hopper!" Molly finally announced. "His first name's Hopper! Mom, may we call Grammy and see what she'd like his middle name to be?"

Aha, reinforcement. Grammy would be on my side. She'd know just the right words to convince them to set him free and leave them thinking it was their own idea. Why didn't I think of Grammy before? I dialed her number, handed the phone to Molly and smiled.

Two minutes later she gave it back to me. "Grammy likes the name Kermit, like Kermit the frog!"

Thanks for nothing, Gram. Perhaps a bit more directness was in order. I sat the kids down and we admired our frog, his cool green color, his tiny black-bean eyes. Haley had the "F" encyclopedia open and was spouting frog facts at us. Molly wondered if they could find a spider web with a fly in it to feed him.

It was an opening; I jumped in with both feet. "Oh, I just remembered. Frogs won't eat in captivity. If we don't let him go, he'll starve."

Molly wavered a bit, but Haley knew better. She'd seen frogs at the pet shop. They must be eating something there. Maybe I could call and ask them?

I went in for the kill. "Gee, his little heart is pounding. He's scared. I'll bet we look like giants to him."

Haley put her nose close to the jar and peered in at him. Molly wondered out loud if she could teach him to do tricks; he might be good at walking a tightrope. "Mom, could I bring him to school tomorrow? May I take him next door to show Miss Camellia? She loves frogs!"

Hopper Kermit Vader just stared.

That's when Providence stepped in. From outside in the irises, we heard the sound of another frog calling.

"Did you hear that, Mom?" Molly pondered. "That might be his mama."

"Yeah, he looks like a baby," Haley agreed. A moment of silence. "Mom, do you think it would be okay if we just let him go?"

"Well, if *you all* think it's best." I could hardly believe my ears.

As Hopper plopped clumsily down on an iris blade, I breathed a sigh of relief. But not for long.

"Come on!" Haley shouted, "Let's turn over the stepping stones and see how many doodle bugs we can find!" And the Critter Brigade was off again.

Mimi Greenwood Knight

The Storyteller

The older I become, the more I think about my mother.

Ingmar Bergman

It didn't matter who was within earshot or that I'd heard it a zillion times before. Mother was on a roll, telling about a picture they took of me holding up four fingers to show how "big" I was getting. Then she'd describe all the cute things I did.

During high school, I rolled my eyes and cringed at each telling. When I protested, she sighed, "When you're a mother, you'll understand."

During college, I winced but learned to tolerate her reminiscing. As an adult, I learned to smile and shake my head slightly to imply: *Mothers, what can you do?* But she knew what I was thinking and she'd repeat, "When you're a mother, you'll understand."

Okay, I am now a mother.

Recently, I came across the photos of Sarah's fourth birthday party. In one, she's wearing a party hat and blowing out candles. In another, her face puckers with "brain freeze" from the huge bite of ice cream in her mouth. But my favorite is the picture of her dressed like Belle.

Not only had my mother given her the Disney doll from *Beauty and the Beast*, but she'd given her a matching princess gown and crown. Sarah took one look at it and rushed upstairs.

"Mommy, look at me!" she called minutes later. My little princess glided down in full Belle regalia, doll cradled in her arms, and paraded around the room. Then she leaped into her grandma's arms, and their smiles beamed toward the camera—my mother and Sarah.

As I gazed at the picture, I finally understood.

I understood how amazing it is to see my child growing so quickly before my eyes. How she holds my face in her hands to make funny fish lips. How she plays pretend school and orders her stuffed, furry students to sit "criss-cross, applesauce." How she crushes me in a bear hug one minute and pulls away the next.

I understood that childhood is fleeting, and I must treasure these precious moments. After all, someday I'll want to remember them through the telling and the retelling . . . just like my mother did. And when Sarah rolls her eyes and complains, I'll simply smile and say, "When you're a mother, you'll understand."

Eliza Ong

The Little Things

Cherishing children is the mark of a civilized society.

Joan Ganz Cooney

My redheaded sons, Tyler and Sam, were making the morning's rush unmanageable. Even more hectic than usual.

No one had gotten any sleep the night before because two-year-old Sam had been sick. My husband would take Sam to the doctor, so I hustled out the door with Tyler, running late. I couldn't wait to escape to work.

"I love you, Mommy. Have a good day at school." Still clad in his cuddly pajamas, a sweetly smiling Sam waved a chubby hand . . . and nearly broke my heart. I ran back through the garage and gave him a big hug and told him Mommy loved him, too.

As a special-education director, I confer with parents, test students with disabilities and decide what is best educationally. On this same day, I was meeting with the teacher at the State School for the Severely Handicapped and the parents of a child in our district. The agenda concerned a list—a lengthy list—of skills I felt the state school should address with this child in mind.

As the meeting progressed, the teacher questioned the parents. "What if there was only one thing that we could teach your child this year? What would be the single, most important thing you'd want your child to learn?"

"There are many things that we feel need to be addressed," said the dad. I nodded my head in full agreement. "But if we could only pick one thing . . ." he exchanged a long look with his wife, "we'd want our child to learn to sign 'I love you.'"

He went on to explain, "We have had six years of struggles and setbacks. Never, ever has our child been able to communicate 'I love you.' Right now that is what's most important to us."

I sat there, humbled. Three little words. The same words I took so for granted that very morning. And these parents had never heard them from their child.

Suddenly, my hectic mornings, sleepless nights and boisterous boys were a real blessing. Three little words . . . *I love you* . . . were mine for the taking, mine for the listening. Thank goodness I'd listened that morning.

Amy Krause

4

A MATTER OF PERSPECTIVE: BUILDING BLOCKS

Twenty years from now you will be more disappointed by the things that you didn't do than by the ones you did do. So throw off the bowlines. Sail away from the safe harbor. Catch the tradewinds in your sails. Explore. Dream. Discover.

Mark Twain

Lucky Me

Oh what a power is motherhood, possessing a potent spell.

Euripides

"Let us pray," announced the pastor as we bowed our heads.

I pressed my eyes closed, silently questioning, "Why is this happening to me?" Only days before, an amniocentesis test had confirmed that our third child would be born with Down syndrome.

Startled by the sudden noises surrounding me, I opened my eyes to see the congregation filing from the pews. Apparently, I had missed the pastor's final amen. Swiping away a tear, I knelt to grab my purse.

"Sheri." I rose as a hand touched my shoulder. The older woman smiled and whispered, "God only chooses special parents to have children with Down syndrome. Don't ever forget that you're one of the lucky few." She squeezed my hand, kissed my cheek and walked away.

A few months later, a smiling nurse placed Hailey in my arms, and I cried tears of joy as I studied my daughter for the first time. My mission, calling and purpose for mothering this little baby became clear as I cradled her. I knew I would shower unconditional love on this special child of God. Fears that permeated my thoughts before her birth were replaced with an inner peace.

"I'm one of the lucky few," I whispered, and a smile stretched across my face.

Hailey is five now. Every morning, she climbs into our bed singing her favorite Barney tune. "I love you, you love me." She grabs our hands. "We're a happy family." She squeezes us tight. "With a great big hug and a kiss from me to you." Hailey kisses our cheeks and finishes triumphantly, "Won't you say you love me, too?"

And even as I try to sleep through another verse . . . and another, I envision God looking down from heaven with a smile asking, "Hmmm, which family needs a special blessing in their life?"

God chose me to be Hailey's mother, our family to be her wholehearted nurturers. He knew ours was the perfect home for a child with special needs. And we try not to disappoint him. We support her; we encourage her; we shower her with an abundance of love.

Each time Hailey smiles into my eyes and says, "Mom, I love you," I reply, "I love you, too." And I am reminded of how fortunate we both are to have each other. The purple dinosaur words sing true, "We're a happy family." One of the lucky few.

Sheri Plucker

One Day, Some Day

What may be done at any time will be done at no time.

Scottish Proverb

Picture this: a box that contains all the times your children have asked you to do something. "Can we go fishing?" "Can you play Barbie dolls with me?" "Can we have a dirt-clod war?"

Typically, my response is, "Someday."

Can you imagine your child coming to cash and claim all those Somedays?

Picture this: a box that contains all the Somedays you've promised yourself. "I will get in those jeans again." "I will run an eight-minute mile." "I will lose ten pounds." "I will clean my refrigerator shelves . . . someday."

Now, imagine this: Life comes full circle—and now it's your children who are making the promises. "I'll come see you soon." "We'll have lunch together sometime, Mom." "We'll plan a trip your way . . . someday."

Some day, these Somedays will add up until one day, Someday will be too late.

Too late to make mud pies. Too late to play dolls and dress up. Too late to run an eight-minute mile. Too late to go to lunch with your mom.

Let's vow to seize the moment. Let's promise to agree. Let's start answering, "Okay. Yes. All right."

When? Someday. Someday really soon.

Lisa Moffitt

Taking Account

"It's starting to sprinkle, Annika. Let's go in," I said, preparing myself for a barrage of objections at disrupting her backyard playtime.

The sky darkened, but the disappointed look on my four-year-old's face dissolved into one of revelation. She turned to me with her rosy, plump cheeks and pleading blue eyes and squealed, "No, Mom. Let's go up in my play-house to get out of the rain! Please?"

Now, keep in mind this is a child's playhouse— definitely not a structure made for adults, never mind a five-feet-ten thirty-five-year-old. Five narrow ladder rungs lead to a four-foot-square wooden platform covered by a roof, a *low* roof. Yet, as the sprinkles turned into large raindrops, the practical, no-nonsense side of me gave in.

"Okay, Annika, let's go!" We dashed to her playhouse and clambered up the ladder into the cramped space.

While water dripped on our heads through cracks in the roof, we talked and giggled, oblivious to the rain. My daughter discovered a new, more playful side of me, and I relived the carefree times of my childhood.

Annika shared her hopes, her dreams and her fears, opening up in a way she hadn't before. Maybe it was the close quarters. Maybe it was because—for those precious thirty minutes—I was totally and completely focused on her, without the usual distractions and clutter of life. No ringing phone, no barking dog, no sink full of dishes.

No worries. Only the two of us, wrapped in each other, safe from the world and its storms.

Although our cozy time in the playhouse happened almost a year ago, Annika recently said, "Mom, do you remember that day it was raining and you climbed into my playhouse with me?"

"Yes, honey, I remember." I listened as she excitedly recounted our entire conversation from that afternoon.

"Mom, that was really fun," Annika concluded.

"Yes, sweetie," I acknowledged truthfully, "it really was."

And I'm making certain our future holds more of the same.

These days, this once-upon-a-time, no-nonsense mom is more apt to roll in the grass with the kids than vacuum or dust, balance a checkbook or pay bills. I'm more inclined to give my undivided attention, for even just a few minutes. And that suits me just fine.

After all, the dividends and interest I receive make it a wise investment.

Cindy Gehl

Off the Mark *by Mark Parisi. Reprinted by permission of Mark Parisi.* ©1994.

On the Run

Some are kissing mothers and some are scolding mothers, but it is love just the same.
Pearl Buck

"Three blind mice. Three blind mice. See how they run."

Forget the blind mice. I had three little boys and, well, I knew how they ran. All over the place. Okay, the littlest guy mostly crawled. But that was enough to make life pretty hectic. I didn't have a moment to myself.

Dirty diapers. Skinned knees. Spilled juice. And the incessant motor sounds of cars, trucks and motorcycles that a house full of little boys make. Sometimes, our household felt like a *Saturday Night Live* version of *Mr. Rogers' Neighborhood.* The stress was getting to me. The insignificance of it all was almost killing me.

Such was the state of my mind one afternoon as I loaded all three boys and drove into the heart of Surrey, British Columbia, to Helen's apartment. We loaded her and her wheelchair into our ancient Honda Accord and headed to a shopping center—handicapped accessible, but in a rough area of the city.

We drifted from shop to shop. The baby slept in the stroller and Nate held tightly to my pants, but my oldest, six-year-old Josh, dashed ahead to the next store.

"Mom," he yelled from just inside the door, "we gotta get these police hats. They're really, really cool." He grabbed a black helmet from a wire bin and stuck it on his head.

When he saw the hats, Nate let loose of my pant leg, put his thumb in his mouth and reached for one. While I saw to a suddenly crying baby, Helen wheeled near the bin and rifled through it. And Josh continued his enthusiastic campaign to purchase his hat. The baby's loud cries competed with Josh's running commentary for my attention.

Helen glanced up. "Hey, where's Nate?"

I looked down, half expecting to see him holding my pant leg. For once, he was not there. Alarmed, I shoved the stroller—and Josh—into Helen's care while I scanned the small novelty shop. Nate was nowhere.

"Did you see a blond boy holding a London bobby hat?" I asked the girl behind the counter. Even before she finished shaking her head, I raced out the door.

Frantic, I searched store to store, begging for news of little Nate. One of the clerks called security. My desperation was chilling.

"Anybody see a little boy? Blond hair? Green eyes? Anybody? *Anybody!*"

But Nate was gone. Vanished. There were no best-case scenarios. Someone had snatched him, and they were probably already out of the building. My mind raced with imagined details.

What about locking down the mall? What about . . . ? There was no time to waste. I turned back to the store. While Helen wheeled up and down the halls, I ran with the stroller and Josh, searching wildly for my little lost boy. It was my darkest of nightmares.

Nathan. Gone. I desperately wanted to turn back the clock and change the outcome. *If only, if only, if only* pounded through my mind with each slap of the stroller's wheels.

"Hey, Mom," Josh shouted as he jerked at the stroller, "mall police."

I slowed as we approached a group of security guards huddled together. One spoke rapidly into a walkie-talkie. Another held a black object. My eyes widened, and my legs wobbled. Tears spilled down my cheeks.

It was a toy bobby hat.

"We found this a few moments ago," a security guard said. "Do you recognize it?"

I nodded, unable to speak. Josh reached up to hold my hand.

"We've called the police," the guard assured me, "and . . ."

Someone touched my shoulder. "Excuse me," a cheerful voice said.

Choking down sobs, I turned to face a middle-aged woman—with a chubby, blond, green-eyed Nate in her arms.

"I found him in the food court at the other side of the mall," she said in a neighborly tone, "calling for his mommy. He pointed. . . ."

I didn't hear the rest of her explanation. My sight, my hearing, all my senses were filled with the presence of the little boy I thought I had lost. He leaned toward me, wrapped his arms around my neck and buried his face in my T-shirt.

"Thank you," I mouthed through tears of gratefulness, "thank you so much."

My Good Samaritan smiled a warm, knowing look that had to have come from her own journey through motherhood.

How long ago was it that I had felt so stressed with the

busyness of raising small children? A lifetime ago? Eons? *See how they run, see how they run,* indeed. My perspective now changed. The baby in the stroller; the little boy tugging at my sleeve; the blond child clutched in my arms. *Did ever you see such a sight in your life?*

And I hugged them to me, these three busy little boys.

Renee Hixson

"Is this one of those times that I'm supposed
to hold your hand or disappear?!"

Play-Doh Perfection

Play creates order, is order. Into an imperfect world and into the confusion of life it brings a temporary, limited perfection. The least deviation from it spoils the game.

Johan Huizinga

There's something about Play-Doh that makes playtime exciting for little kids. Maybe it's because they can shape it and mold it, and each time it becomes something new and different. Maybe that's why my children, Christina and Joseph, love it so much. Or—maybe—it's because they can make a mess, squishing and bending the clay while relishing its nonconforming nature.

Since we go through so much Play-Doh, it was a waste to continue buying globs and globs of it. It would be more frugal, I decided, to make our own.

My creative mission began by searching the Web for an easy recipe. Many required oil (too messy) or cream of tartar (an ingredient I didn't have). At last, I found a great recipe using only flour, salt, water and food coloring.

I rounded up my kids.

"Christina, you're in charge of pouring one cup of flour into each of these plastic tubs. Joey, you put the salt Mommy gives you in the tubs. I'll add the water and dye. Then, we each stir a tub. Ready, crew?"

"Yes!"

We measured.

We poured.

We stirred.

But chaos soon got the best of my efficient plans. Flour powdered everything. Salt crunched underfoot. Joey rolled himself like a pretzel onto the grains of salt strewn across the floor. Christina, pretending to be a baker, patted him down with flour. They laughed hysterically.

"Okay, that's enough!" I said. I stripped Joey to his undershirt and wiped flour off Christina's blouse before shooing them from the kitchen.

"But, Mommy, we need to play with the clay now," pleaded Christina.

"Me, me, me, play!" Joey mimicked the same imploring tone as his big sister.

"You can play with it *after* I clean up this mess. Don't touch the clay yet or everything will get yucky." I bagged each colored mound to keep it clean and prevent it from drying.

"Why will it get yucky?" asked Christina.

"Because it will get full of this extra flour and salt and be messy."

"Whyyyy?" repeated Joey.

"No more whys." I ordered Christina to run upstairs with Joey for clean outfits while I tidied the kitchen.

"But then can we play with clay?" asked Christina.

"As soon as I'm done cleaning. I promise."

Christina raced upstairs with Joey scrambling after her.

It took four sweepings to get the floor clean, but I was able to scrub the table free of caked flour with only three washings. Just as I called for the kids, the doorbell rang.

"It's Auntie Roxie!" Christina shrieked in delight.

"Roxie! Roxie! Roxie!" said Joey.

"Well, since Auntie Roxie is here," I took advantage of the surprise visit—and my sister, "she'll play with you while I do the laundry." She could supervise their Play-Doh time.

But I wasn't ready for the sight that met me when I returned to the kitchen.

"Now look what you've done!" I scolded. "I worked hard to make this with you, and now all the colors are mixed up. Why did you have to waste it all?"

Annoyed at my sister, I reprimanded, "Roxanne, did you have to let them use the entire clay in one day?"

"Oh, don't worry. It's only clay," she replied, unaffected by my growing annoyance. "Don't make Christina feel bad. She was just playing."

"Yes, but she doesn't care or respect the time it took to make the clay."

"Let it go," Roxie replied.

"That's it!" I turned to the kids. "I'm not making any more Play-Doh with the two of you."

"I'm sorry," replied Christina in a soft voice.

I was tired and frustrated—and I knew I sounded like a child myself. Deciding to put some space between us, I walked into the living room to sort the day's mail.

"Auntie Roxie," I overheard Christina say, "doesn't the clay look beautiful? Why is Mommy mad that I mixed it together?"

"Well, Christina, your mommy's not an artist."

"You mean like me and you?"

"Yes."

"Of course, it's easy for her to be an artist," I mumbled under my breath. My sister had no children and was an artist by profession. She didn't deal with the everyday frenetic chaos of a toddler and a preschooler.

Later, while Joey napped and Christina watched her favorite video, I went to the kitchen to start dinner. On the counter, I found a remnant of Christina's Play-Doh.

"They forgot to put it all away," I complained to myself. Feeling a little guilty for my earlier attitude, I paused and began shaping the soft mound. Then I tore away a piece and discovered a swirl of marbled colors.

As a truce, I took it to my daughter. "Hey, look, Christina. I found some more of your clay, and I think it's pretty inside."

"Oh, Mommy, you're lucky now."

"Really, how is that?" I mused.

"Well, see where you opened it—that's the magic rainbow I made for you."

Sandra Giordano

Wishful Thinking

Love is, above all, the gift of oneself.

Jean Anouilh

"The Christmas tree is *soooo* much bigger than last year!" Jeffrey sing-songed in five-year-old fashion, dancing around the beautifully wrapped gifts. He turned to me, his chocolate-brown eyes reflecting the tree's blinking lights. "Isn't the tree much bigger and more beautiful than last year's, Mommy?"

"It is a much bigger tree than last year's tree," I agreed. At least, that's what I'd been told. Christmas 1985 was not even a memory for me. I had undergone two spinal-cord surgeries that year, and I didn't have any recollections of the holiday.

A tabletop tree was all that my husband, Walter, had been able to manage. He tried to make it festive, but it had been difficult for both of them. But this year I was home, and we anticipated a festive Christmas for 1986.

After months in the hospital and rehab center, I had looked forward to life-like-it-used-to-be. Instead, I encountered reality and disappointment—in myself. While I was still making progress, it was slow, and I was not nearly where I had expected to be in my recovery. I wished things could be different. I wished everything could be as it once was.

With these thoughts in mind, I rose slowly from my chair and made my way to the stairs. Jeffrey stopped singing, and I knew he was watching me as I struggled to climb the steps. I heard quick little running steps, and he grabbed my hand to help.

He looked up and said in all solemnity, "Sometimes I wish it was me."

Gripped by the power of his words, I hugged him tightly, burying my face in his wavy brown hair, squeezing my eyes shut to fight back the tears.

"Oh, no, Jeffrey, no!" I interrupted.

"But, if it was me," he insisted, "you could carry me up the stairs." His eyes brimmed with tears as he looked down at the floor. "I can't carry you."

His poignant, generous words jolted me like nothing else could.

In an instant, my introspective melancholy dissolved to a deep sense of gratitude and love. No, things were not the same as they once were—maybe they never would be. But now I realized just how unimportant that truly was. Especially in light of Jeffrey's unselfish thoughts. Finally, I felt at peace.

I looked at the glowing Christmas tree. "You know, Jeffrey, I believe you're right. This year's tree is bigger and more beautiful than any other."

Donna Lowich

Wheels

What can you do to promote world peace? Go home and love your family.

Mother Teresa

There they go again—our neighbors—dashing off in their new convertible Corvette Stingray.

And here I am, like Gladys Kravitz from an old *Bewitched* episode, peeking through my slightly opened front curtain. But this time, I'm not alone. My husband, Dan, hunches behind me, and though I hear his heavy sighs and understand his longing, I can't seem to muster the same level of envy.

Maybe it's because Dan is a car-man. Since he built his first go-cart in junior high, he's dreamed of owning—not a Corvette—but a pristine muscle car.

A shriek from the kitchen catches my attention, and I dart away to avert a potential snacktime squabble. When I return, Dan is still peering at our neighbors' empty driveway. Part of me wants to comfort him, tell him to hold onto his dream and assure him it will happen some day.

Another part wants to remind him that our neighbors

had their children a lot earlier than we did. When they were in their early forties, they were sipping champagne at their children's graduations; we're still weaning ours from sippy cups.

Those are the facts. I'm not complaining. We both know that for the foreseeable future, all of our "extra" money will be spent, not on trips or cars, but on preschool tuition. Then dance lessons. Then college funds. And though he fantasizes about being carefree, I think Dan is quite happy.

Still, it never hurts to check.

"We have a good life, don't you agree?" I ask with raised eyebrows.

"I know that," he grins and turns to hug me. "Did they tell you they were driving down the coast, all the way to LA? Imagine the warm sun on your skin while the wind whips through your hair for an entire day."

He is teasing me now. I stifle the urge to point out that the back of his head is still peeling from his last encounter with the sun and his hair is no longer plentiful enough to "whip."

Four-year-old Alexandra emerges from the kitchen to inform us she cannot eat her cereal because it is too "melty" and that her two-year-old sister, Sarah, has made a hat from her peanut-butter toast.

My husband doesn't move. He just shakes his head and glances at me with a tired, almost pleading look that says, "It's your turn."

Sometimes Dan and I wonder what it would be like to have the energy of twenty-five-year-old parents. Other times we forget that we don't, and suffer the consequences—like last week when Alexandra couldn't get the hang of cartwheels. She had tried so hard for so long that I felt compelled to demonstrate.

"I'll show you, sweetheart. I used to do them all the time." I cleared the room of toys, got a running start and executed a pretty good turn. But, as I landed, my chest constricted, my shoulders throbbed, and my head pounded with the force of a jackhammer.

"Why is your face so red, Mommy?" She touched my flaming cheek. "Don't worry," she added before I could speak, "it's probably just 'cause you're old."

Perhaps I am too old to do cartwheels. But I'm not too old to be a parent. In fact, for me, this is a good time. I am significantly more patient and focused now than I was in my twenties. I'm also comfortable with the conclusion that I cannot have it all, at least not all at once, and I don't even want to try.

But there are a few things that Dan and I do want. When the time comes, Dan wants to be able to walk his daughters down the aisle, without mechanical assistance. I want to change my grandchildren's diapers before someone is changing mine. And we would both like to have holiday dinners at our house, and not at "the home."

And if, while he can still drive, my husband could somehow afford his dream car—a vintage 1970 Buick GSX Stage 3 Ram Air convertible—well, that would be icing on the cake.

Sheree Rochelle Gaudet

5

LAUGHTER IN THE CHAOS

Sometimes the laughter in mothering is the recognition of the ironies and absurdities. Sometimes, though, it's just pure, unthinking delight.

Barbara Schapiro

This is the perfect watch for mothers.
Every day has 36 hours.

Red-Faced and Remembering

Children are a gift from the Lord; they are a reward from him.

Psalm 127:3

I had a mother and her preschooler in my office this week. In the middle of our conversation her son abruptly announced that he needed to use the potty. The mother directed her son to the restroom just outside my door, and we continued our relatively serious discussion. After a few minutes, the boy returned to my office and enthusiastically declared, "The plunger sticks to the wall!"

Stunned, the mother and I looked at one another for a moment without saying a word. As her child's statement sunk in, I held my breath, attempting to stifle my laugh. The red-faced mother looked at me sheepishly, and I couldn't maintain my composure another second. I burst into laughter.

My own son recently turned fifteen. (It's amazing how quickly Big Wheels are exchanged for automobiles, and nursery rhymes are swapped for rock music.) I spent his entire birthday reflecting on precious memories of similarly embarrassing, but equally hilarious moments.

When he was three, my husband and I invited over friends who had a daughter the same age. While the adults conversed in the living room, my adventurous son and the agreeable girl emptied a jumbo-sized jar of petroleum jelly on their heads "to make shiny hair."

Another time, our little entrepreneur gathered acorns from the oak tree in our front yard and sold them door-to-door for three cents each. Remarkably, our lighthearted neighbors bought every acorn his pudgy hands could carry.

Yes, I know the sheepish look of that young mother all too well.

I know, firsthand, that mothering preschoolers can be frustrating at times. But how I wish I'd known then how much I would treasure the memories of my son's antics now. Perhaps I would have found more relish in hugs, more delight in kisses . . . and more laughter in greasy hair!

Mindy Ferguson

The Race

You can learn many things from children. How much patience you have, for instance.

Franklin P. Adams

"I want fish crackers!" Casey whined when he saw scrambled eggs, cinnamon toast and orange juice.

"Fine." I caved without an argument today; I had to be at work by 9 A.M. to finish a project. Handing him the box of crackers, I turned up the volume on the television, and the theme song of his favorite cartoon flooded the house. Casey rushed to the living room, squealing in three-year-old delight and clapping his hands.

"Now, watch your show while I get dressed," I said.

Balancing on high heels, I applied makeup. Just as I leaned closer to the mirror to apply mascara, Casey shoved me from behind. The applicator slipped from my hand and left a trail of Blackest Black across the counter before skidding to a stop in the sink.

"'Scuse me," Casey giggled, crawling over, through and around my feet. Fortunately, my stockings proved to be run-resistant as advertised. Never mind the snags from curious little fingernails.

"Now, let's get you dressed," I urged, knowing it would require several minutes merely to choose the day's underwear. After a detailed debate on the various celebrity characters featured on each pair, he settled on . . . red. His favorite color.

Glancing at my wristwatch, I grabbed a short-sleeve shirt, perfect for the weather, and yanked it over his head.

"Noooo!" Casey's whine signaled trouble. After some confusion and a bit of frustration, I understood that he preferred a long-sleeve shirt.

"But, Casey, look at the pretty fish on the front of this one." I used my motherly wiles. "What could you name a fish?" I edged toward a pair of blue jeans. "How about Fred?"

"No," he grumped.

"Spotty?" I scrambled to put jeans, socks and shoes on him. In protest, Casey went noodle limp and collapsed to the floor.

Still racing the clock, I managed to get us both to the car, hoping I would make it to work on time. As I leaned over to buckle Casey, a pungent odor assaulted my senses. I looked him in the face and wrinkled my nose.

"I have to poop," he said. It was too late. Amazingly calm, I urged him back inside for a change of clothes: clean underwear—blue ones, he decided—and fresh jeans.

This time, we made it as far as the daycare parking lot before Casey whined again. But inside the classroom door, a real battle of wills started when he clung to me, refusing to join his classmates on the colorful floor mats. Countless hugs, kisses and assurances later, he chose to let me win. This time.

One hour late to work, I poured myself a cup of coffee, but my hands trembled as I raised it to my lips. I took several deep, calming breaths and reminded myself to stay focused. Shoving my guilt to the back of my mind, I envisioned a happy, healthy Casey having the time of his life while he learned numbers and letters—then I worked right through lunch to meet my deadline.

That night, a freshly scrubbed boy placed both hands on my cheeks and pulled on my face until we touched forehead-to-forehead.

"I'm gonna marry you, Mommy," he whispered sweetly.

Instantly renewed, I kissed the tip of his nose while a million emotions raced through my mind. As I tucked the covers under his chin, I vowed to relax and enjoy my son more. From now on, it would be fish crackers for both of us.

Natalie Bright

When It Rains, It Pours

Other things may change us, but we start and end with family.

Anthony Brandt

Lauren and Andrea were born thirteen months apart.

There were two of everything—youth beds, carseats, tricycles, near-naked Barbie dolls. And when it happened that four little knees scraped simultaneously on pavement, there was only one Mommy. Taking one by the hand and carrying the other, I brought the girls indoors to clean their bruises before applying ointment and cartoon Band-Aids.

"When will it go away, Mommy?" I heard as I dried their tears.

Channeling my own mother, I answered, "Don't worry. It'll go away by the time you get married." I smiled and kissed their boo-boos, just as my own mom had said and done when I was small.

I dressed them in similar outfits, Lauren wearing her favorite color, pink, and Andrea in "pupple," as she would say. And so it was on a warm, humid July morning that I helped the girls dress and combed their hair into short pigtails with obligatory pink and purple ribbons. Because rain was predicted, I planned a day of chores.

Toting laundry down and up the stairs, I checked on the girls between changing bed sheets and folding towels. Once when I peeked in, I saw Lauren, four, with a pair of plastic scissors; three-year-old Andrea held a blonde Barbie in place.

"Oh, girls, no! Don't cut Barbie's hair!" Lauren froze, mid-snip. I squeezed my awkward, eight-months-pregnant body onto one of their playroom chairs and took Barbie from Andrea's hands.

"Girls, Barbie doesn't grow hair like you and me. Our hair is always growing, so we need to have it cut sometimes," I explained. "Barbie is a dolly. If you cut her hair, it won't grow back." I looked at each girl in turn. "And then her hair will be ugly for the wedding when she gets married to Ken."

Mission accomplished.

Even at their tender ages, my girls knew that every bride is beautiful, and Barbie should not be denied. The girls glanced, almost apologetically, at their tuxedoed Ken dolls sitting stiffly against Barbie's pink house. Lauren put the scissors down. Out came the coloring books and crayons, and I left them to play again.

Ten minutes later, I stepped back into the playroom and found Lauren, again, with scissors in her chubby little hand. And there was Andrea, looking like Rod Stewart on a great hair day—her wispy bangs now half-inch spikes. Beside her left ear, a chunk of chopped hair dangled. My daughter now had one sideburn.

Obviously, I had underestimated the precision of round-tipped toy scissors. Irritated, I collected all play-room scissors, scolding all the while. I then instructed my hairdresser-wannabees that they were never to cut *any-thing* but paper again.

Outside, the sky had darkened, and the house took on a dreary cast. It began to rain and thunder. "C'mon, let's all take a nap together." We climbed the stairs, shuffled through my bedroom doorway and settled in the big bed. They took turns feeling my belly move and picking out names for their mysterious sibling as I sang a quiet lullaby to all three of my children.

"Mommy!" Andrea called through my dream. "It's wainin' in the titzen!" A soft touch brushed against my arm, and I opened my eyes. The girls stood alongside the bed.

"Wake up, Mommy. It's wainin' in the titzen." Then, clearer, "It's raining in the kitchen!" as Lauren, wide-eyed and smiling, echoed her sister.

As fast as possible, I waddled down the stairs. It was indeed "wainin' in my titzen." Pouring, in fact. A lone Barbie shoe floated by.

"How in the world . . ." I realized it was coming from above. Back up the stairs, in the bathroom, I found a running faucet and an overflowing, stoppered sink with two rubber duckies bobbing along its rim. Slip-sliding my big-bellied self across the waterway, I turned off the faucet and pointed sternly toward the girls' bedroom.

They ran.

And I went to the phone to call their daddy home. "Bring a big mop and take-out for dinner. Now!"

That night, I tucked them in, turned on their nightlight and retired to my own bedroom when I overheard my girls talking.

"Lawen, I like the way you cut my haiw today," said a sleepy voice.

With a squeal, Lauren replied, "You look silly, Andrea."

"I know," she admitted, "but it's gonna gwow out by the time I get mawwied!"

Maria Monto

"Relax mom . . . it's macaroni."

Market Madness

My children . . . have been a constant joy to me (except on the days they weren't).

Evelyn Fairbanks

For me, there is a thirty-minute window of opportunity on any given day in which shopping can be accomplished in a relatively painless fashion. This golden time occurs when the children have eaten and exercised, and the baby's diaper is clean. More often, I stagger down the aisles as I stuff cheese into the baby's mouth, chase my three-year-old and drag my five-year-old.

Among the many shopping excursions I've sought to forget, one reigns supreme. Shortly after the birth of our third child, I stopped at a local market for milk. This was, of course, the kiss of death, because once in that Bermuda triangle of Pop-Tarts, ice cream and potato chips, escaping unscathed is impossible.

Anton yanked suddenly on my arm, causing me to drop and break a jar of applesauce. Anne got some on her dress and immediately began to writhe and scream. Baby John echoed her crying, and I noticed his diaper was suspiciously heavy. At this point, I observed that Anton had opened a box of cookies and was munching away.

As the volume of John's screaming grew exponentially, I knew he needed to be fed. Here. *Now*. I sat right down and began to breastfeed—surrounded by splattered applesauce, a screaming toddler and a preschooler now eating the peanut butter with his fingers. My entourage clearly disturbed store attendants who asked several times if I "needed any assistance."

"No," I assured with more than a little sarcasm, "I'm just fine."

Somehow, we made it through the next fifteen minutes. I managed to gather enough meal supplies for several days and made it through checkout, exhausted but satisfied with my accomplishments.

"Drive up or push out?" the clerk asked.

"Drive up, please." I dragged my brood to the car and struggled to change John's diaper in the car seat. Afterward, of course, he again wanted to nurse. Anne and Anton got into a fight. Finally, an exhaustive ten minutes later, I pulled up, curbside, to collect my groceries.

"Number twelve," I muttered out the car window.

"Twelve," the teenager repeated. He wore a strange expression. "Just a minute, please." He walked back into the store and returned with an apologetic store manager.

"I'm sorry," he flushed, "but there appears to have been some confusion. Your groceries were mistakenly given to someone else."

"You're kidding, right? You didn't really give away my groceries, did you?" I raised my own voice over the noise in the back seat. At any moment, a group of singing employees was going to rush out and give me a prize for being the fifty-thousandth shopper, or maybe someone was catching this scene for *Candid Camera*.

"Uh, I'm afraid we did. You can take your receipt and go back in and select the same items again."

I swallowed hard.

I looked over my shoulder at my clamoring kids.

I stared past the manager at the web of aisles waiting to snare me once more.

I couldn't do it again. The store manager had no idea what he was suggesting. It was too much to ask. I pulled a scrap of paper from my purse and scribbled hurriedly. "Here's my address. Please mail me a refund."

"Are you sure?"

"Oh, yes." I nodded emphatically. "I'm sure."

Next time, I'd send my husband—who doesn't understand my terror. Of course, there are two fundamental differences between his trips to the store and my own. First of all, he is very organized and always enters the store with a list and a game plan.

Secondly, *he* shops alone.

Caroline Akervik

Mr. Clean

Laughter gives us distance. It allows us to step back from an event, deal with it and then move on.
Bob Newhart

"Mommy, I'll help," offered my middle son, Andy. "Want me to clean the van?"

"That's great," I thanked my four-year-old. As the young mother of five active children, I welcomed assistance wherever I found it. "Sure, why not?" I approved with only a moment's hesitation.

A joyful Andy set to work.

He dragged the vacuum to the carport. He gathered grocery sacks to collect loose toys and garbage bags for candy wrappers and dirty tissues. And he slammed the house door—both coming and going—as he set about his self-appointed task.

Thirty minutes later, Andy bounced into the house. "I'm all finished, Mommy." He tugged my arm. "Come see the van!"

As he dragged me outside, Andy admitted he did have one problem.

"What?" I asked.

"The vacuum bag broke open and sprayed dirt all over the van," he sighed in disgust. "But don't worry, I fixed it."

He pointed, "See, I took the garden hose and washed it all out."

I looked—and gasped.

The custom-finished interior of our big white van dripped in water. Plush, baby-blue carpeted walls and floor oozed. Upholstered captain's chairs . . . color-coordinated velvet curtains . . . all flooded.

But—discounting the pools of water—the van was as neat as a pin. Andy had done the job he set out to do.

"Well," I tried to ignore my rising hysteria, "you got it clean, all right!" I encouraged the chuckle I felt and let it float to the surface and gurgle out. Soon, laughter flooded my dismay.

The rest of the day, I soaked up water with bath towels and left the doors wide open. It took weeks to totally dry out. Admittedly, the van was never quite the same; eventually mold took over in places where water could hide.

But now, twenty years later, Andy still works with vehicles: He's an elite technician for a Mercedes-Benz dealership, where he has the trust of customers and service managers. He is a master at what he does.

And I'd like to think I played a tiny role in that. After all, instead of being a wet blanket, I managed to overlook the flood and see the rainbow. Perhaps that's what gave him the confidence to try and succeed.

Rita M. Pilger

Story Time

I thought my mom's whole purpose was to be my mom. That's how she made me feel.

Natasha Gregson Wagner

Although my husband usually reads the bedtime story while I clean up dinner, when he's out of town the responsibility falls to me. Not that I don't embrace every waking moment with my children . . . oh, no, not at all.

Okay, let's get real. Some days are easier than others to appreciate the dynamics that define parenting, especially when every limb is being pulled on, clung to or hung from . . . by all my children . . . at the same time.

One cold January night, I was on bedtime duty and wondering why the Olympic committee doesn't award gold medals for parenting. Earlier in the week, I had recommitted to a routine at the gym after, oh, let's say, a year of serious muscle atrophy. Severe pain was an understatement of my physical condition that night. In fact, I found it excruciating to sit or stand.

But life goes on.

After tub time, I gingerly pried myself from the bath

floor, hobbled to my son's room and eased into the story-time chair. Seconds later, life flashed before my eyes when my toddler and kindergartener made synchronized swan dives into my lap. Seventy pounds of squealing childhood landed firmly on my exercise-challenged legs. I gasped at the pain, desperately choking back a not-so-motherly expression.

They squirmed. They wriggled. My eyes rolled back in my head as I moaned and gritted my teeth. "Sit . . . still," I exhaled the words.

At last, they settled into position against my chest, and we read the evening's book-of-choice. In fact, we read book after book after book. I relaxed into their bath-warm little bodies and laughed when they giggled silly questions, pointed out pictures and gave unique commentaries on each page of each story.

Suddenly, I felt another twinge of pain. But this one was in my heart.

Time had stopped for a few seconds, only to remind me it was fleeting. I reflected on the splendor of holding my little ones and nurturing them through these tender years. My throat tightened as I thought about the not-so-distant future when they outgrew cuddling and bedtime books.

I knew that no matter how much I might feel stretched like a rubber band, I needed to treasure the hours and days with my children. And, that very minute, I made a vow to look beyond the "pain," make the most of this time and treasure the moments. These all-too-fleeting moments.

I was struck by the bitter sweetness of this memory-making thought, and as I tucked them into bed, I realized a new story had been written. Indelibly. On my heart.

Sherrie Peterson

Taming Temper Tantrums

Total absence of humor renders life impossible.

Colette

At age five, my grandson, Michael, was prone to temper tantrums. Even Grandpa and I couldn't dissuade him from yelling and screaming and crying when he didn't get his way. When our daughter-in-law, Maria, turned to us for help, we conferred with our friend, Ernie, a retired child psychiatrist.

Maria embraced his advice and immediately put it to use.

Before spending an evening with friends, she took Michael to his room and insisted he throw a tantrum.

"What?" Michael's brows shot up.

"I want you to get angry and start screaming. You have ten minutes before we leave, so you'd better get started."

"What?" Michael asked again, wrinkling up his nose.

"Well," Maria explained, "we're going to be with friends tonight, and we all want to have a good time. I don't want you to spoil our evening or your fun with Timmy. So, I want you to have a temper tantrum. Right now. Then you don't have to do it later."

Michael shook his head in disbelief.

"Go ahead," she urged. "You have only eight minutes left. I'm timing it. So, start screaming."

Michael started to giggle.

"Hurry up, Michael. Scream. Holler. Cry. Roll around on the floor and kick. Just do it! Hurry, we don't have much time left."

Michael doubled up in laughter . . . and his mother did, too.

Maria repeated the technique several times over a few weeks. No more temper tantrums. Now instead of saying, "If you don't stop crying, I'm going to give you something to cry about," Maria says, "If you don't start crying, I'm going to give you something to laugh about!"

Kay Conner Pliszka

"How could I get up on the wrong side of the bed?
It's against the wall!"

Gunning for Perfection

*You have to love your children unselfishly.
That's hard. But it's the only way.*

Barbara Bush

Seven—that's how many times Pete and I moved in our first ten years of marriage. But the last was a dream-come-true: We purchased a four-acre, lakeside lot in Buffalo, Minnesota, the exact kind of rural environment where we longed to raise our three young sons.

We planned and plotted our new home and put special thought into our idea of a perfect kitchen. We wanted it to be a gathering place, accommodating friends and family. Large, with an open countertop overlooking the lake, it boasted efficient stools for conversations, snacks and homework. Another terrific feature we incorporated was a large, tiled island in the center of the room.

Of course, unpacking boxes and setting things straight in my new, ideal kitchen was top priority for Move Number Twelve. It was like putting together a large puzzle as I organized each item in its rightful place. Perfection!

The next day, I helped six-year-old Cole unpack his

room while Kane, two-and-a-half, and Clay, one, enter-tained themselves. As we worked feverishly at our task, we heard the little ones laughing and playing. But after a time, my "mommy alert" went off.

As I rounded the corner to check on them, I saw a grin-ning Kane perched on a kitchen stool—fully armed with his weapon drawn. In his hand was the spray nozzle from the sink hose. The ultimate water gun.

And Clay was his moving "target."

Seeking shelter behind the large island, a giggling Clay peaked out to toddle back and forth just often enough to be shot—drenched—by Kane. Of course, the rest of the kitchen, my perfectly brand-new dream-kitchen, was equally soaked. Water stood nearly a quarter of an inch deep on *everything*.

My gut reaction was to scream at the top of my lungs, "What are you two doing?" Thankfully, however, the humor in the moment was contagious. What a sight! The boys were having the time of their lives and loving every moment of it. Besides, it was, after all, only water.

All three boys helped me mop up. And when we were finished, we nestled next to each other on the cleanest kitchen floor in all of Buffalo. *Ah*, I hugged the boys close, *perfection!*

Rochelle Nelson

A Higher Perspective

Any mother could perform the jobs of several air-traffic controllers with ease.

Lisa Alther

I pulled the van into the parking lot of our towering church and paused in the chaotic midst of four rowdy children, as I do every Sunday.

Please, Lord, give me the strength to endure the stares and raised eyebrows of my fellow parishioners. Just for the next hour.

Sunday services aren't an easy task with my husband deployed overseas. I thought it might be better if I spared everyone the grief and simply mailed in my weekly contribution for the next six months. But I suppose the love of a good challenge keeps me attending in spite of the kids' complaining, tired whining and inevitable restlessness. Besides, it is an important time each week for our young family.

As the church bells chimed a hymn, I herded my little ones through the big doors.

"How is everyone today?" The priest's glance swept the five of us. Six-year-old George and five-year-old Carolyn smiled shyly, but nearly three Sean wrinkled up his nose and hid behind my skirt.

"Good morning, Father," I said.

But out of nervous embarrassment, I kept my head down as we located our usual seats near the rear of the church—where we could make a quick exit if necessary. Baby Sophie—already needing a nap—shrieked as I pulled off her coat. The noise bounced off the walls of our cavernous sanctuary. I felt my face flush.

As the service began, somebody needed the bathroom. Sean, the one who couldn't go by himself. It was the typical quandary. Do I leave the other kids and take him myself, or trust George to escort him?

I took a small leap of faith. "George, please take Sean to the bathroom," I whispered. The two noisy little boys made a rowdy exit, and I waited anxiously until they returned.

"Mom, now I need a 'nack!" Sean announced loudly. I obliged with a handful of Cheerios to keep him quiet. Instead, he pulled a small dump truck out of his pocket, filled it with cereal and careened it—complete with action sounds—across our pew.

Casting a quick glance at the other parishioners, I cautioned, "Sean, you need to be quiet, or I'll take your truck."

He wrinkled his nose and kept playing. Obligated to follow through on my threat, I confiscated the toy.

"AGGGHHHHHH!!" Sean flailed and drummed his heels against the seat. I thrust the truck back into his hand and slid low in the pew, hoping no one would know he was mine.

George hummed loudly and played with his tie. Carolyn lifted up her dress to admire her new underwear. Queasy with embarrassment, I hissed, "There will be no doughnuts today if you do not behave!"

Just then, the organist cued a few chords and the crowd

rose. Singing is my favorite part of the service because its volume drowns out my children's. My own voice rang as I wallowed in the few minutes of peace.

As soon as we sat down, Sophie started to fidget . . . then whine . . . then scream. She gargled as she flung her head back, kicking her legs. She sounded like Chewbacca.

I handed her to George so I could nab Sean, who had bolted down the aisle toward the altar. I snatched him and tucked him under my arm, scissoring his legs and wiggling for freedom. I tried to hold up my head as I marched back to our pew.

What must people be thinking? Mortified, I thrust my children back into their coats. We fled out the door and back to the van.

Church, for us, had lasted twenty minutes.

The following Sunday, George asked if we could sit in the balcony. With some reluctance, I agreed. We filed up the steps and sat down. And throughout the service, I made some surprising discoveries.

When Sean got bored, he could play on the carpeted floor. Sophie could crawl around in relative freedom. George and Carolyn could peer over the railing and see everything happening below.

And so could I.

From this vantage point, I observed the other children in the church. I saw screaming babies, willful toddlers and rambunctious preschoolers. I saw fidgeting kids and restless mothers.

But it was what I *didn't* see that made the biggest impression. No one judged. No one stared. No one seemed to mind in the least that babies cried or small children tired. And I realized that people probably hadn't been critical of me and mine, either.

As we filed from church that day, an elderly woman bustled over. "Honey, you have such a beautiful family!

How do you keep them so well-behaved?"

I beamed, head held high. "It must be the higher perspective," I said. And I proudly marched my children through the door. Skipping toward the car, the children shouted, "Yea! It's doughnut time!"

Jennifer Oscar

6

TIME OUT!

There is . . . nothing to suggest that mothering cannot be shared by several people.

H. R. Schaffer

"Actually I only come here to lie down.
I can't get any rest at home."

"Be" Is for Bunko

It's the friends you can call at four A.M. that matter.

Marlene Dietrich

We call ourselves "The Bunko Babes."

Once a month, we gather to eat sinful foods and pour out our hearts. Oh yeah, and we squeeze in a few minutes of rolling the dice, so we can tell our husbands that we are getting together to play Bunko. See, the guys can understand that. They get together to play poker, to shoot pool, to *do* something.

They wouldn't understand our need to get together just to be. To be called our given name rather than "Mommy." To *be* dressed in clothes free of mashed banana stains. To be in the presence of other females who can feel our pain and celebrate our joy. To be ourselves while we share dreams, pet peeves and our latest war stories from the frontlines of motherhood. To *belong* to a group.

We enter an inviting home filled with scented candles and soft jazz floating from family room speakers. Freshly baked desserts greet us as we mingle in the kitchen. After several minutes of playing Bunko, several hours of chatting and several helpings ingesting hundred calories of desserts, we wrap ourselves in our coats and venture back to our respective houses.

Once home, I quietly sneak into my house, black except for the lone kitchen light left on by my husband. I hear the quiet whisper of the furnaces as I tiptoe over scattered Barbies on the family room floor. I check on my sleeping angels and readjust their covers. I tiptoe into my bedroom, where I'm greeted by my husband's rhythmic breathing.

As I remove my makeup, I notice a new sparkle in my eyes, absent earlier when I scrubbed crayon off the wall and folded my fourth load of laundry. I see a refreshed, vibrant woman looking back at me—a woman ready to tackle another day of crazy, unpredictable parenting. A woman eager to *be* a mother again.

Thanks to "The Bunko Babes."

Tessa Floehr

We Interrupt This Parent

The quickest way for a parent to get a child's attention is to sit down and look comfortable.

Lane Olinghouse

Sometimes my kids are so intent on what they're doing that I couldn't get their attention if I walked across the room on my hands with my hair on fire.

This morning, after my husband went to work, I wandered through the house picking up clutter while my three kids played happily, or at least quietly, nearby. Reaching beneath a couch cushion I pulled out our well-worn copy of *The Runaway Bunny*. One glance at the cover, and a warm feeling washed over me. How many times have I snuggled a sleepy little urchin and recited those familiar words? Suddenly, that's just what I wanted to do. The clutter could wait.

I found my preschooler, Hewson, on the back porch trying to fit a twelve-inch cat into an eight-inch bucket, far too busy to sit still for a book. Haley, age nine, and Molly, seven, were flopped across Haley's bed, playing with plastic horses.

"Look what I found, girls," I announced. "Shall we read it?"

Always the diplomat, Molly replied, "Uh, we'd love to, Mom. Maybe later."

As I sulked out of the room, the phone rang. On the other end a friendly, familiar voice bubbled, "Hey! Been thinking about you!" I opened my mouth to answer and heard World War III heading my way.

"Mommaaaa!" Molly stormed into the room with her sister in hot pursuit. "Haley traded that horse to me for her brown one. Now she wants it back!"

I flapped my arms wildly and pointed to the phone.

"Well, her brown horse was broken, and she can't trade a broken horse for a brand-new one!" Haley whined.

The person on the phone said something inaudible just as Hewson came in, screaming. The scratch across his chin told me the cat had won.

"Gotta go!" I managed to gasp into the receiver. "Let me call you right back."

Fifteen minutes, one adhesive bandage and some intense equine negotiations later, I remembered the phone and realized I had no idea who I was supposed to be calling back. But at least things were quiet again. Time for coffee and a glance at the mail. I sneaked to the coffee pot, poured a steaming cup and unashamedly heaped in two spoons of sugar. I'd earned it!

Then, as if on cue, came another wail. "Mommaaaa!"

This time it was a happy voice. "Come see how high Molly can jump on my bed. She can touch the fan!"

With a regretful glance at my coffee, I darted for the bedroom. "Sweetie, that's not a good idea," I cautioned. "Beds aren't for jumping on. You might . . ."

Crash!

Ten minutes later, I stared longingly from the rocker, where I was consoling Molly, to my coffee on the kitchen counter. It was cold by now. But at least a child was finally in my lap listening to *The Runaway Bunny.*

The rest of the day followed the same pattern. Ten times I announced I was going to take a bath—I even managed to run one—but each time I suddenly became the center of attention. That's how it is when you're a parent: Get on the phone or open a book, and you're instantly the most popular person in town.

By the time I needed to prepare dinner, the kids were absorbed in a television show. I sneaked the phone from its cradle. "I was just imagining you sitting in your quiet house all alone reading a good book." I fished for a little sympathy from my mother-in-law.

She listened patiently as I babbled, then said, "You know, the only thing harder than a house full of kids and no time to yourself is waking up one day to realize they're all grown and you have nothing but time."

The words had barely left her mouth when I heard the stampede heading my way.

"Mommaaaa, we're starving!"

I had to smile at the wisdom of a woman who's been where I am now and survived to tell about it. I hung up feeling reminded that I am indeed the center of my children's universe and just where I want to be.

But in case I ever forget, all I have to do is dip my toe in the tub and wait for the inevitable sound of "Mommaaaa!"

Mimi Greenwood Knight

Down and Out

Thursday meant Mother's Day Out. My three pre-schoolers would go to the church where blessed baby-sitters ministered to harried mothers like me, in need of errand-running—free from strollers, whining and endless trips to the potty.

After putting my two oldest children on the school bus, I calculated an hour to change diapers, wash faces, comb hair and dress the other three. At last they were ready, and I secured the baby in his carrier.

"Okay, let's go," I called. Walking past the kitchen, I spotted my three-year-old on the table elbow deep—*both* elbows—in the economy-size grape jelly jar. Groaning, I set the baby down, snatched my son off the table, held him over the sink and sprayed him off.

As I picked up the carrier and herded everyone down the hallway, I tossed a rueful glance at my reflection in a large mirror. Who was that woman? Dressed in a baggy sweatsuit, hair pulled back in a haphazard ponytail, no lipstick, no earrings. Before preschoolers, I wouldn't have considered going out in public looking like that. I shrugged and wiped grape jelly off my cheek.

On the way to church, the sour smell of spit-up assaulted

my nose. Before preschoolers, I wore the fragrance, "White Shoulders." Now I smelled like parmesan cheese.

In the parking lot, I unloaded the kids, and with the baby carrier hanging on my left arm and the five-year-old hanging on my sweatshirt, I took my three-year-old's hand and trudged up the church stairs. Quite a workout. Before preschoolers, I exercised in a gym.

As the children ran to their respective rooms, I glanced at my watch—9:00 A.M. I had till 3:00 P.M. to accomplish my long list. I gave a gusty sigh. With all I had to do, Mother's Day Out seemed more like Mother's Minute Out.

But as I turned to leave, I noticed a colorful gift bag on a table by the door . . . with my name attached. Curious, I peeked inside and discovered a white mug with tiny yellow rosebuds scattered around the middle. Printed on the rim was a little duck.

The note read: *To a wonderful mother who deserves some time to herself. Go home, enjoy a cup of tea with your favorite magazine. Today is your day.*

Without warning, tears welled and slid down my cheeks. Someone understood. Even though being a mother was what I always wanted to be, it was still hard, often thankless, work. An anonymous person reminded me that, although I wore many hats—wife, mother, daughter, friend—underneath was a woman with needs as well.

I looked again at my list—nothing there that couldn't wait. Orange-spice tea and a *Southern Living* magazine on the front porch were suddenly my priorities.

Perhaps, from now on, Thursday would be *this* mother's day *off*.

Linda C. Apple

It's All in the Timing

If you can give your son or daughter only one gift, let it be enthusiasm.

Bruce Barton

Almost anybody will tell you that the payoff for your parenting is the wraparound hug of an adoring child. What they neglect to mention, however, is the typical timing of such affection.

Children do not need hugs while you're watching them play quietly. Children do not need hugs when you're trying to reassure in-laws that you're doing a great job. Children do not need hugs when you yourself would appreciate a warm embrace.

Children need hugs when you're carrying a basket of laundry downstairs, someone pounds at the front door and the telephone rings.

"Hold me. Hold me! *Hold me!*"

Children need hugs when you're paying the cashier, the bagger drops half your groceries on the floor and the telephone rings.

"Hold me. Hold me! *Hold me!*"

Children need hugs when the pot boils over, the dog chews on your favorite shoes and the telephone rings.

"Hold me. Hold me! *Hold me!*"

Children need hugs when you finally have the child buckled into the car seat, someone honks for your parking spot and the telephone rings.

"Hold me. Hold me! *Hold me!*"

Children need hugs when the waitress is asking you a set of questions that rivals last year's tax forms, you recognize the person you least want to see walking toward you and the telephone rings.

"Hold me. Hold me! *Hold me!*"

Children need hugs when the person you're talking to just finished cataloging the numerous faults of clingy children.

"Hold me. Hold me! *Hold me!*"

Children need hugs when your partner finally recognizes the importance of romance.

"Hold me. Hold me! *Hold me!*"

Children need hugs when the front of them is covered with vomit, paint or ketchup. And speaking of ketchup, don't even get me started on the timing of children who decide they need to kiss you . . . *"Right now!"*

Stephen D. Rogers

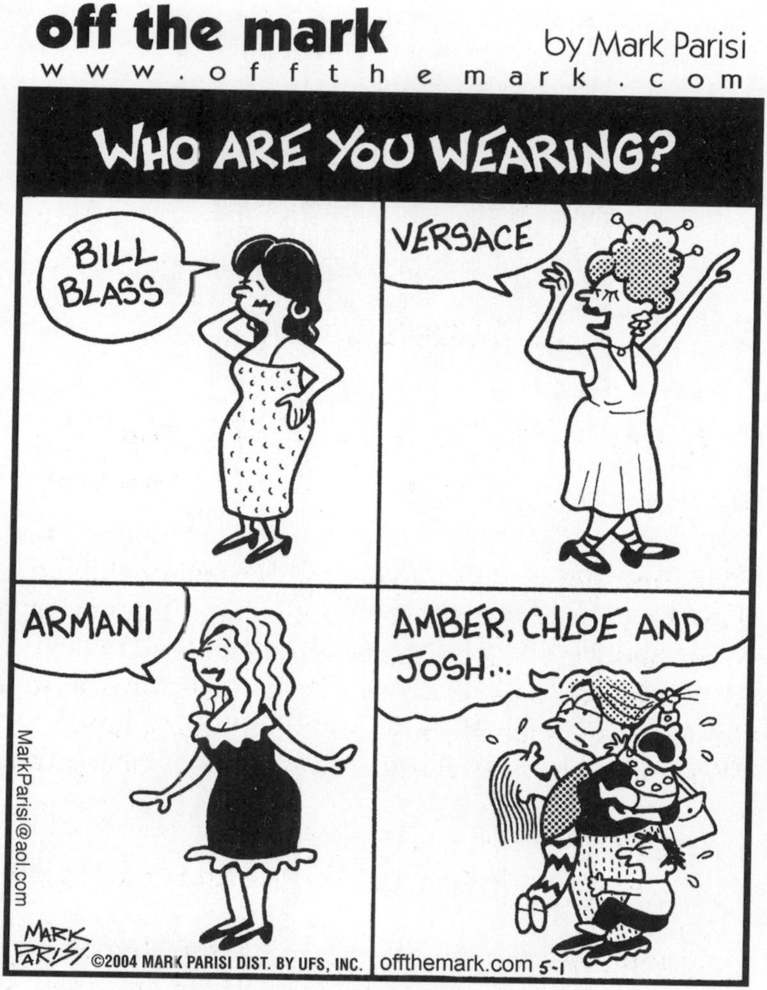

Reprinted by permission of Off the Mark. Mark Parisi. ©2004.

Rosie's Salon

Intense love does not measure; it just gives.

Mother Teresa

"Mommy, get up," three-year-old Rosemary chimed.

I opened my eyes to her face, only inches from my own, and wished I felt half as happy as she looked. I was tired and fighting a nasty cold, and I'd been up in the night with Ryan, five months, who now slept next to me.

What I need, my eyes closed again, *is someone to take care of me for a change.*

"Wake up, Mommy, wake up."

"Good morning, Rosemary," I sighed and crawled out of bed.

"Morning, Mommy." She climbed on the bed and started bouncing. Her face broke into smiles when she noticed Ryan's sleeping body rise and fall with the mattress waves.

"Stop bouncing, Rosie. You'll wake your brother."

"Okay, Mommy." She stopped and started to wiggle instead. I could tell by her impish look that waking her brother was exactly what she hoped.

The last thing I need is for him to wake up before I get a chance to shower. I muttered a bit and tuned the television to PBS. "Here, watch *Dragon Tales* for a few minutes while I shower."

"Sure, Mommy." She plopped down and pulled the covers around her chin.

"And leave your brother alone." She nodded, her eyes already glued to the colorful images of dragons dancing on the screen.

I showered quickly and combed my hair while I peeked around the corner of the bathroom to check on the kids. Ryan was still sleeping. Rosie was rummaging through some toys stashed in the far reaches of my bedroom.

"Look, my Winnie-the-Pooh comb." She held up a baby comb, the kind with extra fine teeth and a cartoon motif on the handle.

"That's nice." Distracted, I thought through my morning list.

Get dressed, fix my hair, put on makeup, change Ryan's diaper, get the kids dressed, eat breakfast, nurse Ryan, feed the dogs, let the dogs out, let the dogs in, clean up, start laundry . . . all before lunch. Then, of course, I had an equally long list for the afternoon. I sighed as I hunted for something to wear. Rosie followed right behind.

"I want to comb your hair, Mommy."

I turned and nearly tripped over her. "Watch out, Rosie!"

"I want to comb your hair," she repeated sweetly.

"Rosie, I have so much to do. . . ." I saw her bright blue eyes and the way she grasped the comb in her fingers. A few minutes of bonding, I reasoned, would be good for us. "Okay," I relented, "but just for a couple minutes."

Motioning to the chest at the foot of the bed, she was all business. "Sit here, Mommy." She propped herself on the mattress behind me.

I braced myself for some unpleasant tugging and tangling, but, miraculously, her tiny-toothed comb glided through.

"Just relax, Mommy." I let out the breath I was holding inside.

"This won't hurt a bit. It's just a little snaggle." I murmured something in reply and glanced at the clock to see how much time had passed—only a few minutes. I looked at Ryan; he was still sleeping.

Oh well, I thought, *I can sit here another moment or two.* I let my shoulders relax, just a little.

"Sit still," she told me. "Now, turn your head."

As Rosemary combed and talked, my head slouched forward and my eyes drifted closed. I melted into her capable hands. I was getting one of the best gifts of my life, time to relax and just . . . *be* . . . with Rosemary.

All too soon, she stopped. "Okay, you're done."

"Done?" I tried to hide my disappointment.

"All done. Look." She turned me toward my dresser mirror like we were at a fine salon. I looked at my reflection. My face was much more relaxed than it had been half an hour before. My hair, still shower-damp, was hardly changed.

"Thank you, Rosie, I love it." I hugged my little hairdresser. She smiled back, proud of her accomplishment. Soon after, I got dressed, Ryan awoke, and we all toddled down the stairs for breakfast.

It would be great to say that the rest of my day was perfect. It wasn't. Perfection isn't possible when you're the stay-at-home mom of two little ones. And yet, when the dogs tracked mud across the floor, when Rosie spilled her juice on the carpet and when Ryan spit up on me, I approached my challenges refreshed.

Instead of getting upset, I let my mind wander back to my morning at Rosie's Salon. She'd done more than my hair . . . she'd *styled* my attitude.

Myrna C.G. Mibus

Pavement Paradise

N*ot everything that can be counted counts,
and not everything that counts can be counted.*

Albert Einstein

Flit, flit, flit.

My thoughts run randomly across my consciousness
until they cascade into a freefall. My body relaxes as the
cool breeze from the car air-conditioning brushes against
my face. Both kids are taking a nap in the back seat.

My mother runs inside the grocery store, and I lay my
head back for the most rejuvenating part of my vacation.
This trip is about refocusing, relaxing, refueling. In a car
two thousand miles from home, there are no dishes, no
conversations and no commitments. I am taking sanctuary where I find it.

Oddly enough, where I'm finding it is in a parking lot,
surrounded by pavement and the perpetual movement of
strangers coming and going.

You see, I have a problem, and I believe it is not exclu-
sive to me. My life is insane, and there are days I like it that
way. In fact, I actually search out projects to fill my life. I

can't say no, and I rarely pass up opportunities—the curse of so many modern women.

But with a three-year-old and a new baby, I am feeling lost, overwhelmed, drained. Because it is tax time—my accountant husband's busiest time of year—I packed my bags and made my annual trek. Home. To my parents. I vowed to find myself again.

And finally encased in a car with no worldly pressures, I find the asylum I so desperately need. Left with nothing more than my own quiet thoughts, I realize my depression is a mild case of baby blues and will pass, and that sometimes a pavement oasis is as good as a hammock on a tropical island.

An hour later, my mother emerges from the store. When I tell her about my parking-lot paradise, she smiles slyly and replies, "Isn't it wonderful?"

It's then I realize she let me sit there so long on purpose. After all, she recognizes my need to escape. She knows what it means to serve as mother, wife, bookkeeper, friend, manager, dreamer, sister . . . all the roles of fulfilled womanhood.

Even more, she understands the need to replenish to meet those demands.

Rachelle Hughes

On a Role

Be careful to preserve your health. It is a trick of the devil, which he employs to deceive good souls, to incite them to do more than they are able, in order that they may no longer be able to do anything.

Vincent De Paul

Driving them home after a full afternoon together with her grandchildren, my mother-in-law braked suddenly. A speeding car had cut in front of her.

"You idiot!" Her reaction was immediate and forceful.

Flabbergasted at the vulgarity, her three young passengers blurted, "Nana, you said a bad word. That is a time-out!"

An exhausted Nana agreed.

When they arrived home, she diligently reminded them that she did, indeed, deserve a sufficient "time-out." Together, they settled on a full fifteen minutes, and off Nana went—book in hand—to serve her punishment. Fifteen minutes of peace and quiet in the privacy of her bedroom.

Awesome!

We could all learn a lesson from Nana. Moms need time-out, too. We devote so much of ourselves to others that we often forget to take care of *us*. Rejuvenation is vital to our well-being and, let's face facts, feels great. Why not allow ourselves a "girls' night out"?

Let the dinner dishes sit, grab a magazine—one with more pictures than words—and put up your feet. Forego the last load of laundry; instead, sit down and listen to your favorite radio talk show. Put the kids to bed early; take a nighttime shower—by candlelight.

You get the picture. We need to carve out some alone time, a bit of solitude. We will be healthier for it, and so will our families.

Let Nana be your role model. I'll share her. As for me, I'm considering taking up swearing. I figure, if I throw around a few bad words, I'll have to give myself a time-out.

Alone.

In the quiet of my room.

For oh, say, forty minutes. After all, isn't the rule one minute for each year of age? Awesome!

Linda Vujnov

The Sound of Silence

Only a mother knows a mother's fondness.

Lady Mary Wortley Montagu

My daughter has been singing the same song for the last two hours and twenty-four minutes. Or maybe longer.

At first, her singing was adorable. After twenty minutes, it was cute. After an hour . . . I'm hiding in my room with a pillow over my head.

Knock. Knock. Knock.

"What are you doin' in there?" she asks through the closed door.

I'm used to having conversations with my children behind closed doors. Take last night, for instance. *Click.* (That's the sound of me shutting the bathroom door.) Five. Four. Three. Two. One. . . .

Knock. Knock. Knock.

"What are you doin' in there?" my five-year-old yells over the running water.

"I'm taking a bath," I yell back. "I need some quiet time."

Jiggle. (That's the sound of her trying to open the locked door.) "Why?"

"Because I want to."

"Why?" Maybe if I ignore her she'll go away.

Jiggle. "Are you still in there?"

"I think your daddy is calling you," I tell her. Brilliant!

Pitter. Patter. (That's the sound of her running off.) Ahhhh. Silence at las . . .

Pitter. Patter. Jiggle. "Daddy said he didn't call me."

Note to self: Advise Daddy of the diversion technique. "Honey, go play until I get out, okay?"

"Oh-kaaaaaaay." *Pitter. Patter.* Five. Four. Three. Two. One. . . .

"Mommy? Can you put Barbie's dress on her?"

A pink and green mini-dress slides under the bathroom door. This isn't the first time things have appeared under the doorway. Books, notes, M&Ms—I've seen it all. Tonight, though, I hear a noise I haven't heard before.

Scrape. Half of Barbie's leg appears, but the rest of her is having a spot of trouble. "She won't fit!"

There's huffing. There's grumbling. *Cruuunch.*

Barbie's entire leg makes it under the doorway. Her body, I am sad to say, does not.

"Her leg! Her leg! Barbie's only got one leg!" my daughter shouts.

Now the Barbie whose arms the dog chewed off won't feel so awkward, I think to myself.

Sniffle. That's my cue.

Swaddling myself in a towel, I open the door to my daughter holding a naked, one-legged Barbie in one hand and rubbing her eyes with the other. *I guess I'll have quiet time another day.*

But not today. My daughter has been singing the same song for two hours and twenty-*five* minutes now. And I'm still buried beneath my bed pillow.

Crinkle. (That's the sound of a note sliding under my closed bedroom door.)

"Wont tu here me seng?" it says in purple. Too cute.

I open the door to her holding a crayon in one hand and a one-legged Barbie in the other.

"Her leg fell off again." She hands the doll to me and—hardly pausing for breath—skips down the hall, singing "I Like to Eat Apples and Bananas" for the 372nd time.

Quiet time is overrated, I suppose. But maybe not for Barbie. That girl needs all the help she can get.

Mandy Flynn

7

HELPING HANDS

The art of teaching is the art of assisting discovery.

Mark Van Doren

Seasonal Secrets

A mother is a person who, seeing there are only four pieces of pie for five people, promptly announces she never did care for pie.

Tenneva Jordan

I peeked at her every day, holding the slats on my miniblinds just right so the viewing space would be imperceptible. As unerring as the morning paper, she'd shepherd two natty preschoolers into a clean minivan at 10:00 A.M. each day. They always looked Sunday-school neat.

What's her secret? I wondered.

I envied her gauzy dresses, flowing loosely in the breeze. I wanted to feel pretty and feminine and put together again. I probably wouldn't wear wide-brimmed hats woven of sun-bleached straw and cinched with a strawberry ribbon, but I might like to try. My car didn't need to be spotless, but the coffee cups rolling on the floor were talking about starting a union.

After a few minutes, I left my post to go back to the television, back to the baby who was crying once more. I went into the kitchen to warm some tea, disgusted with the mess on the countertops—again.

Lord, can every woman in the world juggle all these balls except me?

One day, more out of anger than curiosity, I pulled my hair into a ponytail and set the baby in her stroller. I made sure I was passing my neighbor's step at ten o'clock.

"Oh, hello!" I blushed slightly.

"How are you?" Her lovely British lilt reflected genuine pleasure.

"Fine, fine," I stumbled. "By the way, um, how do you guys always get out here so early looking great?"

She nodded her understanding. "When Lizzie was born, I never got out the door until *Reading Rainbow* was over, and even then my house was a wreck," she chuckled.

Hmm, I mused, *Reading Rainbow* is over at 11:00. I'm ready around noon, but at least I'm within the hour.

Encouraged, I pressed on. "And you always look so pretty." I gestured at her outfit.

"I started buying these dresses after I had the kids. Loose fit and all, you know," she pulled at the waistband and let it snap, showing me the stretch.

"What about your house?" I pressed on, bugging her further even though my brain screamed, *Let it go!*

"Now that I have more energy, it's not so hard to keep up." She saw my droopy eyes. "But the baby was at least six months old before I kept enough dishes clean to eat the next meal."

We chatted for a few more minutes, and then she left to wherever mothers of older children trundle off on a peaceful summer morning. The baby and I strolled a bit and went home.

Later that evening, Michael stayed with the baby while I went shopping to buy a crinkly, gauzy dress. When I returned, he'd made the kitchen sparkle.

I think I can do this after all.

The seasons passed, and another summer arrived. One day my nattily dressed child and I visited a different neighbor, on the kitty-corner side of my street. We cooed at her new baby. I noticed her graying roots needed color; so did her complexion.

She finally blurted, "How come I'm the only woman who can't keep it all together?"

"Let's sit down on the grass," I suggested, "and I'll tell you a secret."

Sandra Byrd

Hand and Heart

Perhaps parents would enjoy their children more if they stopped to realize the film of childhood can never be run through for a second showing.

Evelyn Nown

A set of handprints bakes in the mud on my front doorstep. I've passed by them several times in the last two days. They're drying nicely.

Most people would probably have taken a hose and power-washed them away by now. Not me. As far as I'm concerned, they can stay right where they're at till the next thunderstorm dissolves and washes them away. They speak a message to me that I'm not in a hurry to forget.

I have a friend who would understand that kind of thinking. In fact, she's largely responsible for birthing it in me. She lives by one simple rule: The state of the kids who live in the house is more important than the state of the house in which they live. She's more into *heart*keeping than *house*keeping. If her family's happy and healthy, her life's a success, and she's thrilled. A clean house, but one containing unhappy residents, would speak nothing but failure to her mind and heart.

My friend speaks from experience when she warns me that all too soon there will be a day when my front step *won't* be covered in sun-baked mud . . . a time when I'll no longer need to wash greasy fingerprints and black smudges off my walls . . . a time when my windows and glass doors will remain fingerprint-free for *days* (rather than minutes) after they're cleaned.

She's taught me to deepen the imprint of those little hands on my *heart,* to carry me through those days when they no longer bake in the sun on my front porch.

Elaine L. Bridge

Holding On

*Do not go where the path may lead; go instead
where there is no path and leave a trail.*

Ralph Waldo Emerson

"Let's take a piece of pumpkin bread down to Gramma
Fran," I suggested. "Who wants to go with me?"

Six-year-old Bryce immediately volunteered, always happy
for a visit with our neighbor at the end of the block.

Bundled in warm coats, mittens and scarves, we were
surprised to find the day's melted snow had formed ice as
the evening temperature had dropped. Our shoes had so
little traction that I regretted we hadn't worn boots. The
light dusting of snow made the hidden ice especially per-
ilous. Holding each other's hand, we minced our way
down the street.

Who-o—o-o-o-o-o-oaaaa!

Bryce lurched as he slipped on a patch of ice. Tightening
my grip on his mittened hand, I struggled to keep him
upright and to prevent myself from falling as he pitched
forward, then back, then forward again. Amazingly, after

several seconds of teetering, I managed to steady him and regain my own balance.

"Whew," Bryce exclaimed. "You almost fell, Mom! It's a good thing I was holding your hand!"

Well, I reasoned, we all lose our balance sometimes. And everybody needs a hand to hold.

Cheryl Kirking

A Little Help Please

When a friend is in trouble, don't annoy him by asking if there is anything you can do. Think up something appropriate and do it.

Edgar Watson Howe

"I need help."

Three little, bitty, monosyllabic words. In fact, my three-year-old can even say them. Well, almost. We are *teaching* him to say them.

You see, Sam starts whining because he is frustrated or because he's not able to do something by himself, and I interrupt with, "No whining. Just say, 'Hey, Mom, I need a little help, please.' See, isn't that better?"

I don't understand why it's so hard for him to say, "I need help." Then it hits me: I haven't been the best role model in this area. Help is good; it is what I do for others, and I'm certain I would have no problem being on the receiving end *if* I really needed it. I just never have. In fact, I didn't see myself as needing help a couple of Thanksgivings past.

My widely spread family gets together only once a year,

and it was my turn to host. Did I mention we'd ordered new floor coverings throughout our house, and the only date the carpet layers had available was the Friday before Thanksgiving? Oh yeah, and the kitchen renovation took a little longer than expected—we were hoping to get it usable and clean by Thanksgiving. And I almost forgot, my second baby was due in two weeks; baby number one was all of twenty-three months.

But I didn't need help. I had it under control. I am the help-*er* not the help-*ee*.

At my MOPS leadership meeting sharing prayer requests, I happened to mention my family arriving and needing prayers for their smooth travel and . . .

"Is your family staying with you?" they asked.

"Yes."

"For how long?"

"They're coming Tuesday and leaving Monday."

"Are your renovations finished?"

"Well, almost. They should be finished by Friday." I made some quick mental calculations. "I'll have the weekend to cook and clean while Sam is napping."

"I don't think so." They shook their heads emphatically.

"Excuse me?"

"Please, just listen, and we don't want to hear anything but 'thank you, that sounds great.' We're coming Monday to clean your house. And, oh," they admonished, "please don't clean *before* we come."

Resisting the strong urge to argue, I acquiesced.

Friday came and the carpet was laid; the kitchen received its final finishing touches. I hoped to whittle away at the clutter and sawdust and debris, but I underestimated my energy level and the amount of work involved. Instead of cooking and cleaning while my toddler napped, I joined him. I began anticipating the help of my friends.

Monday rolled around. My cleaning angels sequestered me down the street. When I returned, I was greeted with a spic-and-span home—and food. Lots and lots of Thanksgiving food prepared for my out-of-towners.

Gulping back the emotion that washed over me, I offered a gracious and humble thank-you from the depths of my overwhelmed heart. When the last angel left, I put little Sam down for a nap, plopped onto the couch . . . and bawled in relief and gratitude.

"I need help." I hadn't said those three little bitty words, the words I was teaching Sam. Nor had I realized how true they were. Yet my friends looked past my superwoman façade, teaching *me* the greatest lesson I've ever learned about receiving help . . . and love.

Libby Hempen

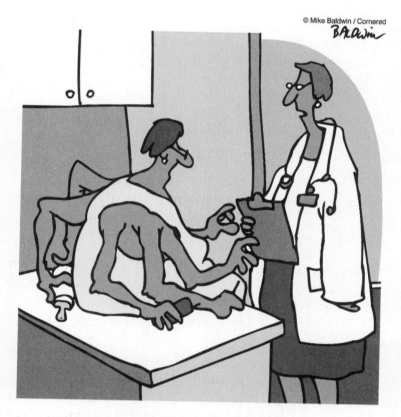

"How long have you been multitasking?"

Daddy Bear

Just the other morning I caught myself looking at my children for the pure pleasure of it.
Phyllis Theroux

"Madison, you need to go back to bed now," I said when she walked into the living room ten minutes after I had kissed her good night.

"But I miss Daddy." Her heart was in her three-year-old eyes.

"Honey, I know you do. He misses you, too."

When my husband joined the Washington State National Guard after college, I never thought that he would actually go to war. I envisioned that he would serve one weekend a month or a couple of weeks out of the summer for a forest fire or other natural disaster.

It simply never occurred to me that I would someday have a yellow "Keep Daddy Safe" magnet on the back of my van, or that he would be a daily target for rocket and mortar attacks.

"But I need my daddy. Iraq is far away." Madison's sweet voice brought a lump to my throat.

"I know." I paused. "How about tomorrow we shop for a special toy that you can hold every time you miss Daddy?"

"A princess toy?"

"We'll see. Now go back to bed, please."

As she trudged off, my heart sank. I knew that she missed her dad very much; we all did. And Madison and Peyton were too young to understand how much their daddy missed them. How difficult it was for him to learn of their milestones and activities through e-mails and broken phone conversations, rather than witnessing them firsthand.

The following day, I took Madison and Peyton to the mall to find that special toy they could hug each time they wanted their dad. Our expedition led us to the Hallmark store where we found a stuffed teddy bear wearing an army uniform. It was soft enough to sleep with, sturdy enough to play with and cuddly enough to squeeze when we were really sad.

"Peyton, what are you going to name your bear?" I asked.

"Buzz Lightyear," he answered.

"That sounds good, Peyton."

"Daddy's helping people," Madison piped up.

"That's right. Do you know where Daddy is, Peyton?"

"In Seattle," he answered innocently.

"What is he doing in Seattle?"

"He's working out."

I laughed, wishing my husband was doing something that simple. And safe.

"Daddy's not in Seattle, Peyton. He's in Iraq." Madison clutched her teddy bear to her chest.

"What are you going to name your bear, Madison?" I asked.

"Daddy Bear." She gave her bear a kiss.

"Daddy Bear," I repeated softly. "That's really nice."

From that moment on, Daddy Bear went everywhere with us. He attended my brother's wedding in Montana, went on a camping trip and joined us on a vacation to Colorado Springs. He slept with Madison, waited in the van while she attended preschool, cheered during her soccer practices, sat quietly in the pew at church, and celebrated birthdays and holidays with us.

Daddy Bear liked to play with princess toys. He was an exceptional student while Madison played school. He was an able block-tower builder. Most importantly, Daddy Bear provided love and comfort to a young girl who didn't understand how much she was sacrificing so that her dad could help people she didn't know and would never meet.

"Madison and Peyton, guess who is coming home tomorrow?" I said.

"Daddy!"

"My daddy's a hero," Madison assured Daddy Bear.

"Like Buzz Lightyear?" Peyton asked.

"Yes, a hero just like Buzz Lightyear," I answered, smiling.

It would be a while before Madison and Peyton would go to their dad with a scraped knee. It would also take time for him to discipline them again.

A lot had happened during the year he was in Iraq. He had experienced a war and would never quite be the same as he was before. We had experienced life without him and would never be the same as we were before. We would try to pick up from where we left off and rejoice in the fact that we were together again, and that he had come home safely.

As I walked through the living room one night, I noticed that Daddy Bear was sitting alone on the couch. I picked him up and headed toward Madison's room. I saw my husband sitting on the bed, with Madison on his left and

Peyton on his right. They pointed to the pictures of the book he was reading and laughed. He smiled and kissed each of them on their foreheads.

I turned and walked back into the living room.

"Thanks, Daddy Bear," I said, hugging him before placing him on the couch and walking back into the bedroom to join my family.

Melissa Blanco

Oh, What a Ride!

Lord, grant that I may always desire more than I can accomplish.

Michelangelo

They were fighting words.

"Do you really think you can handle it?" Nancy asked when we suggested taking two of her sons to a kiddie theme park in Pennsylvania.

"Handle it?" I challenged back. "Didn't we manage to raise three of our own? Are we so old and feeble that we can't be trusted?"

Slightly contrite, Nancy agreed, and we began the actual logistics of this small adventure. Naturally, the day we chose for our Sesame Place outing turned out to be one of those unbearably steamy, early summer days when the sun peeks in and out and the air is dense and heavy. Not a day for perfect comfort with two small lads whose tolerance for discomfort is finite.

We loaded the car with lunch, bottled water, bathing trunks, towels, a stroller for two-year-old Danny, Jonah's favorite toys and several of his most absorbing books, along with some adult gear. Not among our stellar experiences.

"He's bothering me!" Jonah complained while Danny tapped his feet against his car seat for the entire trip, one prolonged by a traffic jam of epic proportions.

"Hungry!" Danny announced as we arrived at the park, along with a cast of thousands. I'd forgotten that toddlers eat constantly, messily and with no regard for food groups. In the blazing sun, with Jonah frantic to get to the main gates, Danny's insistence on lingering over each grape was . . . well, trying at best.

Let me cut to the chase: By the end of the first hour with Jonah and Daniel, who seemed determined to divide and conquer their exhausted grandparents, we were ready to throw in the towel—but it was soaking wet because Danny had thrown it into the wading pool.

By the end of the second hour, with aching feet, burning bodies, the crisis of sunscreen in Jonah's eyes and Danny's terror of the roaming Sesame Street characters, I thought about Nancy's prophetic question. My husband and I were among the oldest people at the theme park, and it showed. While young parents glided through the water and land attractions, we were like cartoon characters run amok. Not a pretty picture.

By the end of our third hour, we did the unspeakable: We lied. We told our grandsons the park was closing for the day.

Hot and exhausted, Danny and Jonah slept all the way home. It was sheer bliss. When we delivered them, Nancy studied her disheveled parents. "So, how was it?"

"Great!" we said. "Really terrific!"

And we beat a hasty retreat before we were caught in our bald-faced lie.

Sally Friedman

Bee Attitude

To be brave is to love someone unconditionally, without expecting anything in return. To just give. That takes courage, because we don't want to fall on our faces or leave ourselves open to hurt.

Madonna

"Mommy, Natasha's in my stuff again!" Cory shouted. "And why does she have to come with us? She's not old enough to go!"

Dashing around to gather items to teach church day camp, I didn't have time to referee another stinging argument. I swooped into my five-year-old's room and retrieved Natasha from a pile of Cory's Lego creations.

"I'm sorry, Cory, but Daddy's out of town this week so Natasha has to come with us today. You can play with your friends. You won't even know that she's there." I took Natasha's hand and led her out of Cory's room.

As the door closed, I heard Cory whisper, "I wish I didn't have a sister."

On the drive to day camp, I mused on my children's

rocky relationship. I had always thought three years would be the perfect spacing between kids. Only one would be in diapers at a time; only one would be getting up at night. But personalities and gender can't be planned. My spirited, outgoing daughter sometimes overshadowed my sensitive, even-tempered son. As I pulled into the driveway, I whispered a quick prayer for a peaceful morning.

Young campers flitted here and there across the lawn like butterflies. Cory and Natasha seemed to be having a good time as well. I gathered all the children to sit on blankets. After taming their wiggles with a song, I began our Bible lesson.

Suddenly, a little boy jumped up, screaming and writhing in pain. A mom cried out, "Bees! Everyone get into the house." Chaos erupted as children ran for safety, crying and holding their hands over stings. Stung several times, Cory ran to me, sobbing uncontrollably. As I tried to comfort him and usher him along with the other children, someone yelled, "Natasha's still out there!"

A glance over my shoulder showed my young daughter stuck in a swarm of angry bees. She screamed and flailed her little hands, but remained frozen in her spot. Not wanting to leave Cory, I frantically called to another mom who raced back and carried Natasha to safety.

Once inside, we surveyed the damages, counted stings, applied medicine and soothed emotions. Everyone would be okay.

That weekend, when my husband arrived home from his trip, I told him about our traumatic afternoon, describing how I had looked up and seen Natasha trapped in the middle of the bees.

Cory clamped his hands over his ears and sobbed, "Don't talk about it!"

I pulled him close and whispered, "It's okay. You're safe.

There aren't any bees here." My husband and I locked eyes in a silent message of concern.

But Cory pulled back from me. "No, Mommy, no." He shook his head adamantly. "I wish it was me." Tears streamed down his face. "I wish it'd been me out there in the bees instead of Natasha!"

And I suddenly recognized that deep inside the heart of my son, a beautiful and sacrificial love for his sister was growing. That's all a mother can hope for.

Andrea Stark

Bearing Thanksgiving

*We make a living by what we get; we make a
life by what we give.*

Sir Winston Churchill

"What kind of Thanksgiving can I provide?" I muttered
to myself.

After all, I had recently moved my three young daughters back to Florida. Living in a small trailer and still job-
less, I struggled to make ends meet.

Still, I counted my blessings when, three short days
before the holiday, I learned that a young family in a
nearby home lost everything to a flash fire. I watched as
the entire community became involved in their rescue: A
church provided shelter; others gathered food, household
items, bedding and clothing. Brigades of busy people willingly gave their time as well as their money.

The afternoon before Thanksgiving, two women came
to our house collecting donations. Although we had little
to spare, I helped carry items to their station wagon, longing in my heart to give more.

As we stood outside chatting, my little Helen, barely

three, shrieked, "Wait! Don't anybody move." She streaked into the trailer door, wailing, "We forgot something!"

I looked apologetically at the ladies, but before I could follow her, Helen was back outside, carrying her favorite teddy, the bear I had made for her birthday just two months before.

"Mommy," her green eyes searched my face, "the little girl doesn't have any toys. She needs this bear. I have to give it to her."

My heart quaked. I thought about the few toys Helen had and how many hours I had spent sewing this one. Now she wanted to give it away. We stood in stunned silence, the ladies staring at me. I struggled with my feelings. I thought of all the things we needed and didn't have.

Everyone held their breaths as I stooped down to face Helen, worry lines creasing the forehead of her heart-shaped face. My fingers brushed aside her red-gold hair even as my eyes filled.

"Of course, Helen," my voice nearly broke, "you're right. We forgot the toy. How thoughtful of you to remember!"

And I realized my own heart would never be as big as the one pounding in my daughter's little chest.

Jaye Lewis

8

THROUGH THE EYES OF A CHILD

Grownups never understand anything for themselves, and it is tiresome for children to be always and forever explaining things to them.

Antoine de Saint-Exupery, The Little Prince, 1943

Of Two Minds

Just like a seeing-eye dog to a blind person is a child to her mother.

Rachel Ryan

Mothers step cautiously around the mud and dutifully check their soles. Children stomp in the puddle and freckle their world.

Mothers look at the blistering sun and moan about the heat. Children drag out the hose and dance under the sprinkler.

Mothers polish their possessions and judiciously store them in their rightful containers. Children lose their toys and sometimes even give them away. For keeps.

Mothers invest and save. Children trade a dime for a penny because it's larger.

Mothers frown at the beat and turn down the volume. Children gyrate and hop, spin and twirl, then amplify the song with their own harmonies . . . and their own lyrics.

Mothers walk by a flowerbed and comment on the choking weeds. Children pluck handfuls of dandelions and weave them into a crown of gold.

Mothers cry accusingly to God, demanding, "Why?" Children just keep praying, "Please bless Mommy and please bless Daddy . . ." and simply blame everything bad on their brother or their sister. Or the dog.

Mothers squish spiders and crunch crickets. Children catch grasshoppers and collect worms.

Mothers look to the future with concern and doubt. Children anticipate *Sesame Street* at 11:30 and remind us about our promise of ice cream this afternoon.

Mothers avoid risk. Children jump from their beds and the top of the stairs.

Mothers shift their eyes from the less-than-perfect. Children boldly ask, "Did God forget to make your other leg?"

Mothers act like the grownups they are. Grownups who have lost the motion in music and forgotten that a crown of dandelions is worth its weight in gold. Grownups who have let their spontaneity rust.

And children act like the children they are. Finding magic in the moment, wonder in the weed and perspective in the puddle. They are earthy and earthly emissaries sent to remind us daily to seek the joy in life.

The joy in living it.

The joy in loving it.

Carol McAdoo Rehme

Meeting Jeanie

As the most recently arrived to earthly life, children can seem in lingering possession of some heavenly, lidless eye.

Lorrie Moore

One frustrating day, I escaped a three-year-old's tantrum and a baby's colic to find a few minutes' respite at the mailbox. I smiled when I saw my neighbor, Jeanie, gliding up, too.

Eighteen years old, Jeanie was born with legs that ended at her knees. In spite of spending her entire life in a wheelchair, she kept a cheerful countenance and a sense of humor. She was a quiet beacon of hope for me. I always looked forward to our short visits.

But this time, I was followed by a preschooler sleuth who had sneaked after me, barefooted on the pavement path. I sighed, irritated. For the first time, I felt a slight amount of trepidation as I faced Jeanie. Would my talkative Hyrum, who'd never met her, feel it his duty to point out her handicap?

I greeted Jeanie when she was a few yards away, and

our conversation began simply and naturally. Hyrum edged along the chain-linked fence, occasionally inserting childishly unrelated topics—our pet beagle, new Buzz Lightyear shoes, the yellow daisies.

Jeanie smiled at each interruption, responding and asking questions. Some of his comments brought a chuckle from her. Simultaneously, she managed an adult conversation with me—a priceless gift to a home-alone-with-children-all-day mother.

I felt my tension dissolve.

We said our good-byes, and Jeanie backed up to leave. Hyrum, however, tossed out a few more comments, reluctant to part. As I scooted him up the path, I breathed a sigh of relief that everything he said had been safe, tactful.

But Hyrum jerked to a stop. "Mommy!"

I looked toward the street and saw that Jeanie was still within earshot. Ready to hush him, I listened as he said, "That was a pretty lady, Mommy! That was a pretty lady!"

Now when I see Jeanie, I never worry about what Hyrum will say. I know that he only sees how beautiful she is.

Tanya Lentz

The Grill Drill

Men are what their mothers made them.

Ralph Waldo Emerson

How does the old saying go? "A daughter's a daughter all her life, but a son's a son until he takes a wife." Whoever coined that phrase was dead wrong. It should go like this: "A daughter's a daughter all her life, but a son's a son until he discovers superheroes and wrestling and baseball." Now *that's* a saying any mother of a preschool-aged boy can sink her teeth into.

And that's exactly how I lost my son. Or so I thought.

For the first year, I was the only one who existed in Weston's world. His round green eyes had only enough room for my face, and he screamed when anyone else dared touch him. I feigned frustration—"This child won't give me a break!"—but secretly I was thrilled.

The second year I became "his girl."

"Don't kiss my girl," Daddy would say, and Weston would run to me, his lips puckered so hard they pinched his face.

"My grill!" he called me, and I blushed with boundless love.

He clambered onto my lap to read books, watch movies, get sleepy, have a snack. But I could see something brewing; he was less baby and more little boy. Losing him was inevitable. And imminent.

Sure enough, age three rolled around, and Weston discovered three things almost immediately: superheroes, rough play and Daddy. Even worse, Mommy wasn't very good at tossing him in the air. She didn't know the Green Lantern from Flash, and, well, she just wasn't Daddy.

At first I got the occasional, charitable snuggle during a Spiderman cartoon and still got embroiled in the "my grill" tug-of-war between Weston and Daddy. But that was simply a precursor to a wrestling smackdown. I was a prop, like a folding chair or a two-by-four.

Soon Mommy vanished from the picture altogether, except to make lunches or tuck him in, and Daddy became a superhero in his own right. *As he should be,* I thought. *But does it have to happen so soon?* I sorely missed the cuddling.

Out of the blue, at almost four, Weston said, "I don't want you to be a grandma."

"Mmm . . ." I said and left it at that, but he became so insistent that I reassured, "But Mommy won't be a grandma for a very long time."

Still he kept it up, creeping up to me at the computer or shouting it out in the bath. "I don't want you to be a grandma."

But why, I wondered, worried that he perceived some defect in my grandma-ing ability. *Doesn't he think I'll be a good grandma?* Finally, curiosity got the best of me.

"Why don't you want me to be a grandma?" I asked.

"Because," he said, his little brow creased with concern, "I want you to stay my grill."

I smiled, fighting back tears of joy. "I'll always be your

grill," I reassured him, and he smiled back at me, relief relaxing his face.

Seems I hadn't quite lost him after all. While Daddy received superhero status, I held a special place in Weston's life, too: I was his first love. My green-eyed baby might have room in his eyes for more than just me these days, but I will forever be front and center in his heart.

It's good to be somebody's "grill."

Jennifer Brown

Spiced Up

A girl is innocence playing in the mud, beauty standing on its head, and motherhood dragging a doll by the foot.

Alan Beck

"The Andersons made this and brought it over for our dessert." I sliced the loaf of zucchini bread still warm from our neighbor's oven.

"This is different from yours." My husband smacked his lips. "It has an interesting taste." I tried it and agreed; it definitely had a different flavor.

Heather, age four, ate bite after bite. "It's delicious."

"Oh, I know," I said after a minute. "It's nutmeg! That's the difference. I don't put nutmeg in mine."

"Nutmeg?" Heather stopped mid-bite. "Nutmeg is in the zucchini bread?" She set the piece back on her plate. "I don't want anymore."

My husband reached for another slice.

"No!" Heather suddenly shrieked. "The Andersons baked Nutmeg into the zucchini bread!"

"Oh, Heather," I sputtered through my laughter, "not

Nutmeg their cat. Look." I opened the kitchen cupboard and held up a small tin. "Nutmeg is a spice, like cinnamon. See, Mrs. Anderson used nutmeg like this."

Heather still seemed a little apprehensive, but slowly finished the zucchini bread on her plate. I cleared the table and began to load the dishwasher.

"Mommy," a small voice interrupted me, "can we go for a walk—and look for Nutmeg?"

Marilyn G. Nutter

"Snow White was poisoned by an apple, Jack found a giant in his beanstalk, and look what happened to Alice when she ate the mushroom! And you wonder why I won't eat fruit and vegetables!?"

When I'm a Grown-Up

When I'm a grown-up
I'll stand high off the ground.
My parents won't nag me
Or boss me around.

I'll run through the garden
And wear dirty clothes.
I'll play in the mud
And put bugs in my nose.

I'll call all my friends
In London and France,
And run through the house
With no underpants.

I'll stand on my head
And look at my toes.
My socks will have holes
And no one will know.

I'll stay in the bathtub
For hours on end.

I'll throw me a party
And invite my best friends.

When I'm a grown-up
I'll stand proud and tall,
And remember the time
When I was just small.

Jodi Seidler

Cents and Sensitivity

With only a few more shopping days before Christmas, my daughter had her heart set on making a homemade gift for her teacher. In spite of my pre-holiday frenzy, I loaded Micaela, five, and Nikolas, three, into the car and headed to the local fabric store.

Keeping an eye on the time, I rushed up and down the aisles collecting the craft items we needed. As I wrote a check for the merchandise, I noticed both kids staring wide-eyed at a display on the checkout counter.

"Mama, who's that?" asked Micaela.

"Where did her hair go?" wondered Nikolas.

I bent low and quietly explained that the picture was of a little girl sick with a disease called cancer. "The medicines she gets from the doctors help her get better but make her hair fall out." I fished in my purse for spare change and let the kids drop it in the box. "The money will help the little girl. Isn't that nice?"

As I held their hands on the way to the car, I thanked God for my healthy children and asked God to bless the little girl and her family.

Next on my impossibly long to-do list, was an appointment and lunch. But Micaela and Nikolas were not so quick to forget the needs of the poster child.

"Why didn't we give her more money?" they asked.

"I didn't have any more change," I answered, "and we still need to buy lunch."

"Hey, let's eat sandwiches at home," suggested Micaela, "Then we can give her the money instead."

"And let's give her all our piggy bank money, too!" Nikolas suggested.

Touched by their sensitivity and unselfishness, I opted to alter our hectic plans and drive straight home. After we ate PB&Js, the kids emptied their banks. Dimes, quarters, nickels and pennies they'd saved for months made an impressive pile on the kitchen table.

"If you give all this away," I cautioned them, "you won't have any left to buy the toys you've been saving for."

"Well, that's okay, Mama. Didn't you see? That girl needs our help!"

We bagged the loose change and headed back to the fabric shop.

Standing eagerly in line among harried holiday shoppers, Micaela and Nikolas smiled and jumped in excitement. When we reached the register, the clerk recognized us. "Do you have a return?"

"No," Nikolas pointed, "we want to give our money to the sick girl."

Stretching on tiptoes, they started dropping their saved coins into the slot on top of the box. One at a time. Dimes, quarters, nickels and pennies. I tossed a worried glance over my shoulder at the long line forming behind us and shifted uncomfortably.

Plink. Plink. Plink.

The clerk, too, realized this might take a while and tossed an apologetic look at the other customers.

But one of the ladies behind us dabbed at her moist eyes and said, "Don't worry, we'll wait. We'll wait."

Unaware of the emotion around them, the kids continued feeding the box. *Plink. Plink, plink, plink.* When their bags were empty, Micaela lifted the cardboard display container and shook it a little. "It's a lot fuller now, Nikolas." She nodded in satisfaction. "I'd say almost full to the top."

Nikolas grinned and gave it a final shake for good measure.

And the lady behind us smiled. "Thank you for letting us watch. It isn't every day we get to see little hearts grow."

Tasha Jacobson

Picking and Choosing

The man who insists upon seeing with perfect clearness before he decides, never decides.

Henri Frederic Amiel

Jessica plants herself in the aisle and inspects the stickers.

We've done this so many times, you'd think she'd have them memorized. The selection doesn't change much— butterflies and Pooh and flowers—but she deliberates as if she's never seen them before.

Maybe she hasn't.

It's difficult to know what Jessica thinks or sees or remembers. I do know that making choices is hard for her. Of course, most things are hard for her. Jessica has a rare genetic disorder that causes seizures, partial blindness and sensory dysfunction.

I don't even remember all the things the doctors have diagnosed; I stopped listening a long time ago. I find choices hard, too, but that was one choice that wasn't difficult to make.

"You need to pick, honey." The frozen french fries in our grocery cart are beginning to thaw.

"Hard to choose," Jessica says.

Indeed it is.

When she was nine months old, the neurosurgeons asked me to choose brain surgery. They wanted to remove most of the left side to control her seizures. No parent should ever have to make that choice, but that didn't stop them from forcing me to make it. When the surgery didn't work, I chose not to sue.

When I chose to leave my husband after years of unhappiness in my marriage, he said, "I think we would still be together if not for Jessica." For all I know, it could be true. But I chose not to blame my daughter for my own failings.

Sometimes it is hard to choose. To remain undecided, uncommitted: I wish I had *that* choice.

Finally, I grow exasperated with Jessica, who stares at the selection of stickers without moving. "Choose!" I command. "If you don't pick right now, we're going to leave without any."

Jessica loses her focus, and I wish I had chosen not to make my threat.

"Mama is mad," she says.

She is learning about emotions and isn't always confident she has identified one correctly. She's not entirely sure what emotions mean, but she knows she doesn't like it when I'm mad.

Her own feelings she keeps to herself. She has an autism-spectrum disorder; I wrote the name of it down somewhere, but the diagnosis isn't helpful. It doesn't tell me what to do or how to parent her, how to reach her or quiet her when she's agitated or keep her from becoming agitated in the first place, how to respond to the cruelty of others who feel threatened by her differences, or how to write my books when I've spent the entire day rocking her in my arms. Mostly the doctors give unhelpful diagnoses and I do the best I can, and sometimes wish I had made different choices.

"Mama is mad," I agree.

Jessica doesn't understand fine shadings like bored, impatient, frustrated. To Jessica, people are mad . . . or not.

"We've been standing here for twenty minutes. Let's go," I say firmly.

"Want stickers!" she wails.

"Then PICK!" I wail.

"Hard to choose," she says.

And I start to laugh. Indeed, it is hard to choose—hard to choose to take the next breath when the neurologist says your newborn daughter's brain is massively deformed; hard to choose to write the next story when everyone rejected the last one; hard to choose to walk away from a marriage to a nice man who never grew up.

Jessica beams when she sees my smile. "Mama not mad," she says knowingly.

"No, Mama's not mad anymore." And I give her a big hug. She pushes me away slightly so she can look up into my face.

"Mama picked happy."

I glance at her, startled. But she has turned back to the stickers, undecided between Pooh and Mickey Mouse.

Pick happy, I tell myself, turning it over in my mind as if it were a foreign concept. I think of all the joy and all the sorrow I have felt since this child came into my life, and I reflect on the irony that she is the one to teach me the answer to the most important choice of all. Even if, otherwise, she finds it hard to choose.

Jennifer Lawler

9

LET SCHOOL BEGIN

A neighbor said that our kids are like birds, and when they learn to fly, we must let them go. So I did. But I have always left a little birdseed out, and they fly back regularly. I am truly blessed.

Beverly Cook

Marker Magic

It's very important to give children a chance.

Nikki Giovanni

When I decided to check out the private kindergartens in San Diego for my pint-sized daughter, Alyssa, I knew she would face an interview at each school. Instead of letting her worry, I explained that *she* would conduct interviews and then tell me what she thought of each school.

Alyssa marched into her first interview with a clipboard and a yellow pencil. On the paper, she had drawn a series of large circles. I smiled and waved at the teacher as she closed the door behind them.

Alyssa's high-pitched voice carried through the partition. "Okay, the first question I have for you is: How do your markers smell?"

I could hear the teacher laughing in response. This was a good sign. I decided to make a chart myself while I waited."

The teacher laughed, recovered and said, "Could you please ask me that question again?"

"Sure," Alyssa agreed. "How do your markers smell?

Does your yellow marker smell like lemons or bananas?"

"That's a very good question." The teacher pondered a moment. "But I don't know the answer. Let's go into the classroom and see." She walked down the hall with Alyssa, who smiled a casual, "Hi, Mom" as they headed to the classrooms. I stayed on my bench, waiting for the verdict. It came about ten minutes later.

"Banana," Alyssa whispered as they returned to the interview room. Her nose wrinkled in disgust.

At dinner that night, Alyssa's father asked what she thought about the kindergarten she had visited that morning. "Oh, Daddy," she said, like he should know the answer already, "the school's yellow magic markers smelled like *bananas!*" She stuck out her tongue.

"So it was a banana school." Her attorney father prefers clear-cut answers to every question.

"Yes," Alyssa concurred, "a banana school."

"Well, you still have seven more to visit." He winked at me.

And so it went at school after school. Alyssa asked the same leading question. Some teachers made up a lame answer like, "They smell nice, Alyssa. Please sit properly on your chair so we can get along with my questions for you today." Others ignored the question altogether. Few bothered to go check. I crossed those schools off my list.

At dinner each night, Alyssa's father would ask about that day's interviews.

"The teacher doesn't know about her markers," she might report.

"Really, really, really banana," she might reply.

A couple of schools got a "lemon" score.

After we'd visited all the schools, I printed out an Excel table that detailed the pertinent facts about each and settled Alyssa on the couch in the living room with her favorite Barney video. Her father and I retreated to the dining-room table where I spread out the school information packets we'd collected.

"Okay, I've analyzed each school in terms of their teacher-student ratio, facilities, cost, distance from home and. . . ."

He held up his hand. "That's wonderful, honey, but all I want to know is whether your top choice is a banana school or a lemon school?"

I swallowed. "It's a really, really banana school."

"A really, really banana school," he repeated. We both glanced at Alyssa, engrossed in Barney's millionth rendition of his "I love you" song. "How are we going to tell her?"

"Don't worry, Daddy," Alyssa called out, her eyes still glued to Barney, "I can bring my own markers!"

Kathleen Ahrens, Ph.D., and Tracy Love, Ph.D.

Back-to-School Q&A

The parents exist to teach the child, but also they must learn what the child has to teach them; and the child has a very great deal to teach them.

Arnold Bennett

It's back-to-school season, which means—besides doing a victory dance—parents are busy, busy, busy.

It's overwhelming, really. There are blue cards, yellow cards and vaccination records. There is glue to buy, new clothes to wash and Superman lunchboxes to be found. There are classroom craft donations to find and collect. There are . . . I don't think there was this much preparation for my first year of college.

My first task to get my son Ford ready is finding immunization records missing since our last move. (Note to self: must be more organized in future.) I am also, unfortunately, responsible for hunting down a Spiderman action figure who "walks with his feet"—the kind Ford's friend Max has. (Because who knows what would happen if Ford started the new school year without a Spiderman who walks on his feet!)

I'm doing all right until the new teacher sends a questionnaire to complete and return.

The first question asks, "Does your child tire easily?" I look up from my place at the kitchen table at Ford leaping through the air, arms outstretched, yelling "Supermaaaan!" I look back at the form, smile and write, "Unfortunately, no."

Question 2: "What is his/her request words for using the bathroom?"

Answer: "Usually just a simple—yet loud—'I have to potty!' in the middle of the grocery store."

Question 3: "Does your child have any problems we should know about?"

Answer: "Depends on your definition. Is calling himself Superman and dressing up in a red cape every single day considered a real problem?"

Question 4: "Does your child have any allergies?"

Answer: "Yes, to Kryptonite. Don't worry; he'll explain."

Question 5: "What type of discipline works best with your child?"

Answer: "If you find one, please let us know."

Question 6: "What holds your child's attention the longest?"

Answer: (Blank)

I zip through the questionnaire until the last demand: "Describe your child."

This, I feel, is a no-win request from parents. Obviously, I think Ford (and his younger brother) is the smartest, cutest and funniest kid on the planet. But I picture his teacher rolling her eyes at yet another student who will be "brilliant and polite," who "read when he was two years old and can already do simple algebra." (Actually, we're still working on tying shoes and not burping at the dinner table. Ford can't read or count to twenty, which is why I'm sending him to school, right?)

So, how am I to answer this question? That Ford says too much too loudly, earning him the nickname "Chief-Talks-a-Lot" in last year's Thanksgiving play? That he sits still for, maybe, two minutes out of every day?

No, no, no. Admitting to all this might get him labeled as the "challenging one."

I struggle with this last question for several days, until at last I have to choose which is worse, describing my child . . . or being labeled as The-Mom-Who-Turns-in-Late-Paperwork. So, what do I write?

Answer: "Just call him Superman, and Ford will be your best friend."

Sarah Smiley

Growing Up

The alarm caused me to leap from bed. There, beside the door, stood my five-year-old cherub. Her golden curls were caught in a lopsided ponytail and on her feet were socks, one blue and one white. But on her face was a look of utter excitement.

"Hurry up, Mommy. I got to go to school today."

It was at least two hours before the school bell would ring. But, no matter, this was her first day. My baby was going to be a big girl.

We ate our cereal and laughed at the cartoons on TV. I dressed and then helped her fix her ponytail and change socks; she decided on Mickey Mouse shorts and a matching top.

As we got in the car, she hesitated. "Mommy, will I like it at school? Will they like me?"

"Of course, they'll like you. You'll have a wonderful day at school. You just wait and see."

I wished I could make it all happen just so, but I knew this was a time for letting go. And it was a *big* letting go. She was my only child and the love of my life. Placing her in the care of people I did not know but had to trust was difficult, and I knew it would be the first of many times. I had enjoyed being at home with her, making sandcastles at the beach, listening to her sing "The Itsy Bitsy Spider" and catching lightning bugs at night.

As we pulled into the schoolyard, I prayed that all those who came in contact with her would believe in her dreams and encourage her, and that she would learn all she could and bless others.

We walked to the front door of the school, hand-in-hand. She slowly released her grip and looked up at me, eyes wide with wonderment.

"Mommy, I'll see you later. I've got to grow up now." And with that, she was off.

Joy and sadness tugged at my heart as I walked away, recognizing the new page we were turning in our lives.

When I got home, I folded the laundry, certain I could still smell Johnson's Baby Powder on her clothes. My mind caressed the memories of her babyhood. Time had passed all too quickly.

I smiled as I remembered her words, "I've got to grow up now." And I realized that as I had let go of her hand that morning, I had placed it in His. We were both growing up.

Marsha B. Smith

"I'm struggling with Empty Pouch Syndrome."

Preschool Pangs

What children take from us, they give . . . We become people who feel more deeply, question more deeply, hurt more deeply and love more deeply.

Sonia Taitz

The door opened with a squeak, and I tentatively peeked inside the brick and concrete building. Once the carriage house for an estate, it now housed the preschool my three-year-old would be attending. I stepped in slowly, still struggling with the idea of leaving my child with strangers for three hours.

Could he handle the separation? I had only left him with family before.

Laughter floated from the upstairs classroom, seeming to gather steam as it bounced off each step. I clenched Nicholas's hand, but he squirmed and broke my hold.

"Use the handrail, please." I tried not to shout. The steps were steep, steeper than ours at home. Would the teachers be as concerned? Would they call me if he hurt himself? Could they comfort him? Tears threatened, but I sniffed them back.

As we drew closer, I secretly hoped we'd gotten the wrong day, or that his class had been cancelled. But as we rounded the corner, the room burst with preschooler energy. Ten children were playing dress-up, coloring, browsing through books—looking like they were thoroughly enjoying themselves.

"Mrs. Yankee, so glad to see you," Ms. Linda, the lead teacher greeted me. "Is Nicholas ready to play?" She smiled down at my son, whose eyes had doubled in size as he took in the room.

Shelves overflowed with bright boxes of rubber balls, colored blocks, puzzles and games. Corners contained cars and trains, dolls and dinosaurs. Tables offered glue sticks, crayons, colored pencils and safety scissors.

"Nicholas," Ms. Linda knelt in front of him, "here's your cubby. You need to put your shoes here and then put on your slippers. Did you bring your slippers?"

"Yep. Look." He pulled them from his backpack and exchanged them for his shoes. "Momma, look who's here!" Nicholas headed straight for his friends—without a backward glance—and was quickly engrossed.

I saw my own friends standing in the back of the room, watching their kids. "Can you believe it's time for this?" I strained to keep my voice level.

"Well, at least it's not kindergarten," one said. We groaned and rolled our eyes, knowing that this separation was only the start.

When it was time for the parents to leave, I spoke to Nicholas. "I'll be back when school is over. If something bad happens, you go see Ms. Linda or one of the other teachers and they'll call me. Okay?" I kissed his cheek and hugged him hard.

"Okay. I'll miss you. You'll be back after I play outside, right?"

"You bet." I gave him another kiss and hug.

"Bye!" Nicholas ran back to his friends.

But I held back a few seconds more, reluctant to leave. It hurt more than I'd expected.

As I descended the stairs, thinking again how I hoped the teacher would bark out orders to hold on to the handrail, I felt at a loss. Now what? I stopped outside of the building and stood in the late summer morning. Birds chirped; a light breeze toyed with my hair.

Memories flooded over me: strolls in the park, pushing Nicholas on a swing, his first ride down a slide. I closed my eyes to see the smiles and hear the giggles. At last, I let the tears flow; they streamed down my face freely, and I wore them like a badge of motherhood.

"What are you going to do now?" Another mother stood near, her own eyes damp.

"I don't know. Go home I guess."

"We're going to Starbucks. Wanna come?"

I looked up at the carriage-house window, heaved a sigh and nodded agreement. I'd be much closer to the preschool at the coffee shop than at home. I checked to make sure my cell phone was on. Just in case.

When I returned for Nicholas, a new fear settled in the pit of my stomach: Would he like his teacher more than me? But out he bounded, arms spread wide, and hugged me harder than ever before.

And I realized that the *real* value of preschool wasn't in blocks and books, puzzles and playtime. It was in the learning: to be apart, to spend time alone. It was in the separation training . . . my own!

Kristine Yankee

Fears and Tears

My mother was the making of me. She was so true and sure of me, I felt that I had someone to live for.

Thomas A. Edison

His face fell as we approached the fingerprint-covered door. Both hands clenched his Hot Wheels lunch bag; his bottom lip pouted.

"Sweetie, you're going to love your new preschool."

I took his tiny hand, soft and unmarred by stresses yet to come in his life. Play-Doh-filled fingernails were still pliable, but his spongy palm would one day be checkered with calluses. His head tilted, just enough to let a corner of his eye peek at me. He saw me looking and turned to stare at some invisible thing on the ground.

I knelt down to his level where massive blue eyes pleaded to me, teardrops building. That bottom lip slipped out further.

"I know you're going to have fun. You're going to have so many new friends." I leaned to look into the class, hoping he would follow. He did not. A tear slid down his chubby cheek. Oh, those cheeks. Rosy, soft and smooth.

I had to toughen up if this was going to work. "Okay, let's go talk to your teacher." I wiped the lone tear. "I'm sure she is going to adore you."

Uh-oh. Hold on now, I thought, *that was a lie. Look at those teachers.*

I could see shocks of gray hair, furrowed scowl lines and courtesy smiles for the parents. Behind them twenty-two Energizer Bunnies bounced off the walls. The sound was sonic: coughing, yelling, crying, sniffing while toys defied gravity. I thought I heard a tiny growl and saw one of the teachers grit her teeth.

Ms. Teeth-grit came over and took my son's hand. He pulled it back and stuck it in his pocket. I kissed his golden curls, nodded to the teacher and stepped to the door. With a squeal, he ran to me and threw his arms around my legs.

"It'll be fine as soon as you're out of sight. It's normal."

Is she nuts? Normal . . . to leave an innocent child in a room of teeth and fists?

I gave him a gentle push, turned and walked away.

The air outside hit me like a blast of disinfectant. But he was back in there, back in the *germ pit.* Tempted to scoop him out of the war zone, I tiptoed around the corner and inched one eye over the windowsill. Window blinds. I couldn't see in. I sighed.

Buckled into my truck, I slipped the key into the ignition and turned the engine over. *What the heck was I thinking?* The engine revved. *Was I insane?* I couldn't breathe. *Was I just going to leave him to the wolves?*

I yanked the key out of the ignition, opened the door and leaped out. Okay, so I didn't exactly leap out. I kind of tumbled and hung out the door, the seatbelt strained. Red-faced, I looked around for witnesses and righted myself. I started the truck and eased the gas pedal.

Time to let go. Time to let him discover the amazing world beyond Mom.

After all, he'd be there only two hours. I drove. It felt good. A deep breath purged all the evil thoughts I had inside, and I . . . simply . . . drove.

Honk, honk, honk!

What is this guy thinking? I pulled over and let the car behind me pass. *What an idiot. Didn't he realize it was a school zone?* I put the truck into reverse and backed into my still-warm parking spot. Okay, so just another hour and fifty-eight minutes.

What do kids do in preschool anyway? My mind wandered a bit.

Wasn't there some show that mentioned child labor? Kids in dark rooms, sewing clothes. The blinds were shut! They're making clothes in there!

I ran out of the truck (this time I remembered to unbuckle the seatbelt), past the blind-covered window. I was sure I could hear the hum of sewing machines, tons of them. No, the sound came from the children. They were singing about a . . . bumblebee. They were covering up the sounds of the toiling tots.

I paused, poised to kick in the door. Just as my foot was about to connect, the door opened to a teacher with children in tow. *Where is she taking them?* Maybe she was going to sell them on eBay!

She walked past with a curious smile. (Of course it was curious; I was about to crack an underground child-labor ring. I was on to them!) They walked to a room down the hall—a sorting and transporting room? A flush jolted me as the kids dawdled back. I was right. They were transporting things out of that room, but not what I thought.

I peered around the doorframe. Not a sewing machine in sight. I saw my cherub; he sat in a circle with the other kids. I analyzed their faces. Were they miserable? Did they look like they were hurt or in pain? Poker faces, every one of them. The teacher smiled and shut the door.

I waited one hour and fifty minutes. The door opened and erupted with smiling, worn-out children. My son was not among them. Adrenal panic. *Where is he?* The teacher cocked her finger and pointed into the room.

Alone in the far corner stood my boy. Seeing tears on his face, I ran to him. They weren't tears; his face was dotted with blue sparkles. He held up a sheet of paper covered with blue paint, glue and sparkled flecks and beamed. "Mommy, I made this for you."

My own eyes welled with tears. My son. I was so proud. He had walked into the room a baby boy and left a budding artist. I thanked the teachers, with their streaks of well-earned gray and eyes framed with smile creases. Hand-in-hand, the two of us left; his other hand gripped the masterpiece that would end up on the fridge.

But I was sure I could smell the faint odor of sewing-machine oil.

Libby Kennedy

Late Bloomers

Hope is the thing with feathers that perches in the soul. And sings the tune without the words, and never stops at all.

Emily Dickinson

We waited in silence, his tiny fingers clutched tightly in mine.

Although the calendar said September, the thick, hazy air felt more like early August. I made lots of small talk about the squirrels playing in the trees and how pretty the bluebeard, sedums and other late-blooming flowers looked as they quietly opened the colorful petals that had been so tightly shut for most of the summer. It was finally their special time, late in the season, to show all their beauty.

Today was the big day, a day that marked another precious milestone in three-year-old Connor's life—the first day of preschool. I was filled with emotions: utter disbelief that my baby was old enough to venture out without me by his side, anxiety and a tinge of sadness because a chapter in our relationship was ending to make room for strangers to enter the story.

My feelings were bittersweet. Yet I knew preschool would start an incredible new adventure in Connor's journey, a first stepping-stone to his future.

I casually glanced at a neighbor a few houses down posing her daughter by a massive oak tree for a first-day-of-school picture. A sky-blue minivan whisked the girl to a nearby nursery school. Other neighbors honked and waved as they whizzed off to their children's momentous first days.

Connor and I continued to wait in the still, muggy air, watching for the little yellow bus provided to "special needs" children. Unlike others his age, my son had absolutely no verbal language. He'd been newly diagnosed with global developmental delay, possible autism.

Connor zipped and unzipped his bright red backpack, over and over again. I chatted about how much fun he would have at his new school; I told him that his teacher, Mrs. Bennett, was nice, that she would take good care of him. He continued fiddling with his backpack in silence.

At last, the bus rolled right up to our house. The wheels squeaked to a halt. Connor barely noticed the large door that swung open to welcome him aboard. Camera in hand, I hoped to snap a quick photo, but—upset as I urged him toward the strange vehicle—Connor threw himself down and cried.

My heart sank like a rusty anchor. I picked him up and lugged him onto the bus, choosing a cracked, green-leather seat near the driver in which to place him. Both the driver and the bus monitor insisted he would be fine, but the bus rumbled down the pavement with Conner still screaming. I waved a stiff good-bye and stood at the end of the drive until the bus was a yellow dot on the horizon.

* * *

But after that, we watched in awe. Like flower petals unfolding to the sun, Connor blossomed.

We noticed little things at first. He climbed up the bus steps on his own. He began waving good-bye from the bus window. And he became deliriously excited when the bus arrived. Throughout the months, his teachers shared ideas to help Connor improve his language and cognitive skills at home. They, too, believed in his ability to succeed.

We took nothing for granted. We celebrated each new word, then small phrases and, at long last, sentences. By the end of the year, Connor was in full bloom—able to verbally communicate most of his needs. Able to engage in pretend play. Able to interact appropriately with others his age. Our "special needs" child now blended with his peers.

Seven years later, he is a bright, curious fourth-grader in a regular classroom. He plays soccer and baseball and hangs out with his friends. Like the late-blooming bluebeard and sedum flowers in our garden, Connor only needed to be nurtured and appreciated as he matured and blossomed in his own special time.

Cheryl L. Butler

Mommy's Help, Er

Never give in, never give in, never, never, never.

Winston Churchill

On the first day of preschool, I gave my child two pieces of advice: Always wash your hands after going to the bathroom, and keep your fingers out of your nose. In hindsight, I wish I'd added a third: Never volunteer Mommy to be a classroom "helper."

Halloween was just days away when I received a phone call from Kate's teacher. My four-year-old had raised her hand when the teacher asked whose parents would like to help with the party. Could I please bring paper products?

It sounded easy enough. I purchased an adorable set of Halloween plates with matching cups and napkins. The day of the party, I proudly spread them on the classroom table.

"Where are the spoons?" asked the mother-in-charge-of-the-party.

"Spoons?" I rummaged through my sack, searching for the "missing" party supplies—and a passable response. "I ...uh...thought I was supposed to bring paper products."

After watching twelve children slurp and lick apple-sauce from my adorable paper plates, I spent the rest of the afternoon wiping twelve adorable chins and dabbing twelve adorable—but stained—costumes with my once-adorable napkins.

Ignorance, however, did not remove my name from the helper hit list. Another request came—this one with more specific instructions: purchase six cans of juice for the hol-iday punch, chill and deliver them to the preschool one hour before the party. If I successfully completed my mis-sion, I'd be given the privilege of pouring.

I bought three cans of red and three cans of green juice and delivered them to the school the next day, wearing a jolly smile and a colorful holiday sweater to camouflage any spills and splatters. Ho, ho, ho.

Without mishap, I helped distribute treats and then headed to the punch bowl, expecting to see a lively red or green brew. Instead, I faced a murky brown concoction and disapproving stares.

"What's this?" I asked.

"Even most four-year-olds know red and green make brown," one mother frowned.

"I thought the children would like a choice," I muttered.

"Choices lead to fighting."

I spent the afternoon pouring brown punch into color-ful cups while listening to twelve children dare each other to drink the "reindeer diarrhea." I knew I'd never be asked again to help with classroom parties.

But that didn't eliminate calls about special projects. A desperate mother pleaded for an extra pair of hands to help the class make cornhusk dolls. No sewing, she reas-sured me, just a little gluing. At last, something I could handle: Elmer and I went a long way back.

I entered the school, full of confidence and was guided to a table and, uh, *armed*. At least, it was shaped like a gun, complete with barrel and trigger. Was this a way of saying I'd better do a good job—or else? Then I was handed some cylindrical tubes. Ammunition?

"It's glue. For the glue gun." One mother demonstrated and explained, "Wait for it to get hot, then gently squeeze a drop onto whatever you're sticking together."

I dripped and drizzled enough glue onto the dolls to fossilize them. Within the first hour, I had glued two kids to each other and my purse to the floor. After gluing the son of the mother-in-charge to the blackboard (by accident, honest), I was dismissed.

Somewhere, I'm convinced, there's a handbook titled: *Unspoken Rules, Regulations and Codes for Parent Helpers.* If only someone would tell me what's in it.

There's so much more for me to learn. That's why I called the mother-in-charge and told her to sign me up as a helper for the rest of the year. Her response?

"Ever consider homeschooling?"

Patricia E. Van West

Special Delivery

Laughter is by definition healthy.

Doris Lessing

I desperately wanted to be a mother. My dream was not fulfilled for five long years.

So, after the miracle birth of our baby—a handsome lad with curly hair like his dad's—we set about with gusto, spoiling our probable only-child. Two-and-a-half years later, a baby brother arrived, and first-son begged Grandma (who had come to rescue us all) to "take that b-b-baby home on the b-b-bus with you."

Exactly two years later, twin sisters arrived, and first-son relinquished all thoughts of ever reigning supreme again. Adding insult to injury, another brother timed his arrival two years after that, the last of our brood.

Well, yes, I had wanted to be a mom, but I hadn't counted on a six-year sentence of nonstop suckling and daily laundry loads of cloth diapers. (No disposables available to us '60s moms.)

Just when it seemed that I had lost my identity, I suddenly found the oldest four enrolled full days at a nearby elementary school and the lonesome-youngest requiring his mom's full attention. All day long. Now I ask, how many times could I be expected to read *The Pokey Little Puppy* with enthusiasm?

In a desperate move to rescue some small part of my sanity, I whisked lonesome-youngest off to preschool, half-days. Though we hugged and I faked a tear, I felt a sense of relief and sudden freedom. I drove my 5,400-pound Buick station wagon home with all the windows down, pretending it was a convertible sports car and that I had long locks flowing in the breeze. In reality, the locks had been shorn years earlier in favor of a short, easy do.

But when I entered our big, empty house, my best laid plans melted away. What would I do with four free hours every day? Music! That would pep me up. Sinatra? Too mellow. John Denver? Too folksy. Classical? Not in the mood. Ah, yes, Neil Diamond, just right for the moment.

As the rhythms pounded out and the volume grew, I found myself dancing with gay abandon. Seized by a sudden, uncontrollable urge, I removed pieces of clothing and tossed them around—in perfect beat to the music.

Knowing my husband's and neighbors' schedules—and not expecting visitors that day—I even liberated my undies. I turned up the volume and pranced through the house singing, "I'm free, I'm really free!"

I danced in the living room. I danced in the kitchen. I danced in the family room, the upstairs hall, the master bedroom and—with a naughty chuckle—I danced in all of *their* rooms.

My over-forty body bounded back down the stairs to the still-pounding music and I arrived at the bottom—just as the doorbell rang. Snapped back to reality, I froze in front of the door, not daring to move since there was clear glass flanking its sides. In my panic, I wondered if the unexpected caller had caught a glimpse of my shameless dance.

I dared not move, even though the blaring music was a dead giveaway that someone was home. I held fast through two more rings of the bell, clinging to the cold wood and hyperventilating. The record finally ended, all was quiet outside, and I heard an engine start.

Shyly peeking around the door through the side window, I glimpsed the UPS truck edging from the curb. I blushed (full-body), swept up my scattered clothes and dressed. Then I turned off the stereo and sat down at the kitchen table to plan dinner.

The next day, I opened the door to a handsome, young, brown-uniformed man—his "second attempt" to deliver. As I signed for the package and he wished me a nice day, I thought I saw an amused glint in his eye. Red-faced, I accepted the parcel and closed the door, feeling in my soul that the two of us shared an unspoken secret.

It was a short liberation after all.

Carita S. Barlow

Hire Calling

Sons are the anchors of a mother's life.

Sophocles

Cuddled beside me on the couch, Donnie asked, "Mommy, what will you do while I'm away at preschool?"

"I'll probably cry my eyes out and eat every M&M in the house . . . then I'll wait for you to run home!" I teased.

Seeing the frown on his face, I assured him I was kidding and would bake cookies instead, so we would have something to munch on while he told me about his first day.

Because my husband was overseas, I walked Don by myself. Fighting tears, I kissed him good-bye.

He gave me a big hug. "Don't worry, Mommy, I'll be home soon. I *know* you'll be okay!"

Time crawled while I got some cookies in the oven, straightened the house and . . . waited. I was at loose ends when I glanced at the clock and realized he'd only been gone forty minutes.

Then someone knocked at the door. A woman about my age stood there with a big smile on her face. "Are you Donnie's mom?"

"Yes," I whispered, gripping the doorknob tight as my mind imagined all sorts of dire things.

"I'm Marilyn," she chuckled. "I met Donnie at the playground yesterday. When I told him I live only a *few* doors from here, he paid me a quarter to stay with you during his first day at school." She dropped a lazy wink. "He thought you might get lonesome and said for me to be sure you didn't eat all the M&Ms."

I smiled back. "So, he gave *you* his quarter instead of the ice-cream man!"

After sharing some laughs, a couple cups of coffee and only a *few* M&Ms with my new friend, I realized my son was growing up, ready or not. After all, he'd interviewed, hired—and paid for—a "Mommy Sitter."

Avagail Burton

10

PRECIOUS MOMENTS

The quality of your life is measured by the little things.

Barbara Braham

The Mom

I looked at this tiny, perfect creature, and it was as though a light switch had been turned on. A great rush of love flooded out of me.

Madeleine L'Engle

"Mom! Mom! Get up!" Four-year-old Madison pats her hand on my bed. "You have to be *Bear in the Big Blue House*."

"Maddy, it's early, honey. Let mommy wake up." I yawn and stretch, really wishing I had another twenty minutes.

"But you have to be Daddy. *Bear in the Big Blue House* is on!"

"Now I have to be Daddy?" All I want is a cup of coffee. "What happened to my being Bear?" I sigh. "How about letting me get dressed first?"

And so my daughter's daily world of magical make-believe begins.

But by the time I get around and am working on that cup of coffee, Maddy—The Director, as her daddy calls her—is focused on princess characters.

"Let's do *Sleeping Beauty*. And, Mom, do the boices." In Maddy's world, everything is possible.

"Maddy, I don't do the voices. Daddy does." *And I wish he was here doing this instead of me,* I complain inwardly.

"Yes, you do," she bellows. "Hit it, Mom!"

Where did she learn that phrase? I wonder, tickled.

Maddy directs. I follow. She insists I do the entire play and be all the characters.

Admittedly, after some practice, I do a pretty good rendition of Sleeping Beauty, Fairy Merryweather *and* the Wicked Fairy.

"Tee, hee, hee," I flutter around the backyard as the Wicked Fairy. "I cast a powerful spell on this child."

"Oh, dear, dear, dear," I pace as kindhearted Merryweather. "However will I break this dreadful spell?"

"Stop, stop, stop!" The Director stiffens her arms and holds out her hands. "You forgot to be The Mom!"

"The mother in *Sleeping Beauty*? What does she do?"

"Come on, Mom, do the part. You know it," Maddy coaxes.

I do? I think hard, but, for the life of me, I can't remember what the mother did in the movie. *I give up!* I concede silently. *After all, I'm not much of a make-believe-world Mom.* And I switch roles . . . to play myself. "Yes, now I'm the mom, and this mom says it's time for lunch and a nap."

"Ahhhh." With a little stomp of her feet and a pleading to continue after lunch, The Director sets down her wand and follows me indoors.

Yet, this time I can't seem to take advantage of the all-to-me hour I always anticipate while my daughter sleeps. None of my projects appeal; I'm not even interested in a friendly phone chat with a girlfriend. Instead, I revisit Maddy's insistence that I play the role of Sleeping Beauty's mom.

"Well," I admit to the empty room, "maybe I need to review the movie." And I pop the tape into the machine to catch that important scene at the beginning.

I watch the Mother Queen cuddling her little daughter in her arms. I listen as she and the king discuss how hard it was for them to conceive a child. I muse over the village-wide celebration they plan for this blessed babe's arrival.

And comprehension sets in. Tears flood my eyes. *I do know the part,* I think. *I am that mom. I live this role.*

It took years and years (and invitro) for my king and me to conceive our blessed daughter. We, too, celebrate her and the joy she brings to our family. And suddenly, I laugh aloud to realize that I do live in a world of fairy-tales—where magical things happen, anything is possible, and I know my part as Mom.

And I live in that world with my very own Sleeping Beauty!

Maria Nickless

Rainy Day Cake

Sometimes the laughter in mothering is the recognition of the ironies and absurdities. Sometimes, though, it's just pure, unthinkable delight.

Barbara Schapiro

"Rain! It's raining!" Shaun shrieks with joy. The sliding door to the back porch reflects a pulsing circle of fog as he presses his face against the rain-swept glass. "Mommy, can we make a Rainy Day Cake?" Shaun begs as he hangs on my sweater.

"Chocolate or vanilla?" I untangle his grasping fingers.

A strong memory from my childhood is the Valentine Cake. I don't know the origin of this family tradition, but the recollection of made-from-scratch, messy, delicious cakes frosted in red, white and pink and covered haphazardly with nonpareils, sprinkles and red-hot candies is one I cherish to this day. The cakes Shaun and I make to celebrate rainy days are equally unprofessional looking: crumbs swirled into the frosting, fingerprint indentations or long swipes where taste-testing occurs.

Rainy Day Cake is nothing if not a production. Flour

swirls through the air; cracked eggs drip down the outside of the bowl. Aprons take on a batter-speckled pattern. Shirt cuffs become encoated as little fingers dip into the bowl for quality-control tasting. The project also challenges my son's still-evolving belief system.

"Mommy, raindrops are blue so we should use blue sprinkles. But . . . my favorite color is red." His eyes seek an answer in mine. He chooses red sprinkles. Is the experience of using red sprinkles to represent blue raindrops a small lesson in the concept of abstraction?

Then there is the agonizing exercise in patience as we wait for the cake to cool before we frost it. Even more difficult is the decision whether to leave it whole to share when Dad gets home or have a piece now. Mom's dilemma is whether to break her diet. Sharing a piece of Rainy Day Cake in fellowship and love far outweighs the actual calorie intake every time.

We sit in the window seat—our "castle"—and watch the rain sheet down as we nibble. Shaun asks how rain is made and if birds can fly in it. He asks when it will stop raining but seems to be quite content in our warm, dry fortress. He only eats the frosting and candy decorations. *Would he be satisfied,* I muse, *with an open can of frosting and a spoon?* I doubt it.

Time to clean the kitchen together. Bowls, pans and wooden spoons are washed; flour is swept off the floor; crumbs are wiped from the counter. Priorities are reviewed as Shaun reflects on the project. "Mommy, I love Rainy Day Cake," he hurries to reassure me, "but I love you more than anything else in the whole world."

Our tradition celebrated again, cake pans are put away until the next rainy day.

Mary Comeau-Kronenwetter

Superheroes

Few things are more rewarding than a child's open, uncalculating devotion.

Vera Brittain

I never saw Spiderman look so good.

In a plot to create a Mother's Day surprise, my eldest son orchestrated a covert gift-making operation. From his four siblings, he recruited the two who don't drool.

Secretly, they filled page after page from their favorite coloring books to create their masterpiece: a Spiderman collage. Their superhero, adorned in a rainbow of colors, is depicted in all sorts of cataclysmic scenarios—battling villains and ensuring that good triumphs over evil.

The pages are ranked according to the artistic abilities of a seven-, four- and three-year-old. Each bears a message—written in varying degrees of coherence—ranging from "Happy Mother's Day" to merely the artist's name, in randomly selected capital letters.

It's adorable. Completely uninitiated and, therefore, all the more cherished.

The kids stowed the pages in a private location,

accessible only by the tooth fairy: underneath their pillows. When the pictures emerged on Mother's Day, they looked, to say the least, well-rested.

I'm a big fan of the web slinger. But that's not what makes the gift tear-jerking precious.

Instead, it's the chubby face with dazzling eyes. It's the dimpled little hands. It's the "Happy Mudder's Day" moment when a wad of priceless artwork was thrust at me—the reason all mothers save yarn flowers, painted rocks and Popsicle-stick crafts. It's that face, that look that says, *For this moment in my little life, you, Mommy, are the most important person in the world to me.*

I dread the day they won't look at me with such admiration, when my loving glances might not be reciprocated. Or the day my man-child looks at "another" woman with admiration and love. And today's handcrafted token will become the souvenir of my past.

But for now, *I* am the object of their affection. Their first love. *Their* superhero. And I'll tuck away my Mother's Day gift along with a piece of my heart.

Besides, a purple and orange Spidey? You can't put a price on talent like that!

Christina Quist

Reprinted by permission of Off the Mark. Mark Parisi.

At Your Service

A happy family is but an earlier heaven.

John Bowring

"Forget about willing us your money," my husband counseled his mother. "As your financial advisor, I'm telling you, if you want to see a huge return on an investment, invest in your family. Why don't you plan a trip and take us all with you?"

Heeding his advice, my mother-in-law mailed tickets to the entire family, scattered from the East Coast to the West. She attached a note that read: "Let's meet in Jamaica and celebrate the New Year together. Love, Mom."

It was our first trip out of the country with three-year-old Zoe, and she couldn't wait to be with her grandma, cousins and aunts.

We boarded the red-eye with two suitcases in hand—a gigantic one filled with toys, books, diapers, sunscreen, floaties and blankies, and a teensy one stuffed with bathing suits and shorts. Zoe stretched across our laps, tossing and turning before finally nodding off. Visions of frosty margaritas and Jacuzzi-warm Caribbean waters lulled me to sleep despite my bolt-upright position.

"I *like* the new place!" Zoe exclaimed upon discovering the basket of sweets and a welcome balloon in our hotel room.

The "new place" was indeed full of wonder. Elevator buttons miraculously turned green at the touch of her fingertips. Messy beds and dirty towels reappeared fresh and clean as if by a magic wand. But nothing surpassed the sheer amazement of awakening to a table of fresh fruit, muffins and warm milk.

"How'd this get here?" She rubbed the sleep dust from her eyes.

"Room service," I said, watching those two words permanently implant themselves in her vocabulary.

"Room service," she repeated, rolling the words on her tongue as if they possessed the same mysterious powers as "open sesame."

Zoe polled every person she encountered on the elevator. "Grandma, did room service come to your room? Aunt Linnie, Aunt Lisa, room service came to us; did they come to you?" And each morning for a week the room service fairies slipped in and out before she awoke.

Our trip ended much too quickly, and it wasn't long before we found ourselves at the airport hugging and saying our good-byes and thank-yous.

Back home, I tucked Zoe into bed. Memories fresh, we reminisced about the trip: playing with Grandma and the cousins, water slides and sandcastles. We made pinkie promises we'd do it again as we kissed goodnight.

I went to my room and found my husband unpacking. "You're brilliant," I said, hugging him from behind. "'If you want to see a huge return on your investment, invest in your family.'" I kissed him. "That's advice I'll have to remember."

At dawn, the alarm buzzed relentlessly, and Zoe

padded into our room and into our bed. "Where's room service?"

"Oh, honey," I rubbed my eyes and chuckled, "room service is *over*. We're not on vacation anymore."

"It's not fair! I want room service!" she wailed. "I *like* room service!"

"Oh, I do, too. Believe me."

She remained inconsolable, and my head throbbed to the rhythm of her sobbing. I desperately needed coffee.

"Wait here. I'll bring you a surprise." I stumbled out of bed and closed the door behind me.

Minutes later I returned and rapped at the door.

"Who's there?" Zoe asked.

"Room service," I said in my best hotel voice.

"Come in," she beckoned. Her eyes lit at the sight of the tray bearing warm milk, hot coffee and books.

"Scoot over." I slipped in beside her, and we snuggled close beneath the feather comforter. Indulgently sipping drinks, we read, laughed and tickled long into the morning.

"See, Mommy," said Zoe, with the divine logic only a three-year-old could possess, "every day is good for room service!"

"You're so right." I smiled.

It's been seven years now since "room service" started. We even fit it in on school days, and we have never missed more than a handful. But it's the mornings when Zoe awakens me—precariously balancing her signature coffee concoction along with books on a tray—that I marvel at the huge and unexpected return on my investment.

Tsgoyna Tanzman

All That Glitters

Whatsoever things are lovely . . . think on these things.

Philippians 4:8

"Don't you just think they are absolutely beautiful, Mom?" Savannah asked.

"Sure, hon." I tossed a distracted answer over my shoulder as I fruitlessly searched for sensible black Mary Janes, girls size ten.

"Oh, can't we get them, pah-leeze?"

I looked into the dancing brown eyes of my four-year-old. Clasped in her hands were white slip-ons, covered in silver glitter. Oh, but what *really* attracted her were the shoes' one-and-a-half-inch heels. My little girl loved to play dress-up.

"Savannah, black shoes are better for church. They go with everything and don't show dirt," I insisted, ever practical.

"I don't like black. It's ugly. I think God would like these sparkling shoes better. It looks like they have been covered in snow." She waved the gaudy slippers under my nose.

Looking at the stubborn set of her chin, I had to admire her defense. Savannah, like God, was drawn to all things lovely.

Realizing she'd gained ground, she cajoled again, "Pahleeze? They've got magical snow on 'em, just like the Sugar Plum Fairy!"

This shopping trip was winding down a rare girls'-day-out to see *The Nutcracker*—her first ballet and a truly special time for the two of us. I melted under the spell of the moment—and my daughter—just like I had so many times before.

The slippers sparked the memory of another day spent together. The two of us were walking through the snowy woods at our country home, admiring winter's beauty.

"Mom," Savannah commented, "it sure has been ugly around here since fall. It's a good thing God made it snow. But do you think he'll get in trouble for dumping glitter all over the place?"

And I recalled the family reunion when someone told her she was growing like a weed. "I don't want to grow like a weed," Savannah had pouted. "I want to grow like a flower!"

And what about last Christmas? When she saw baby Jesus in a nativity scene, Savannah was beside herself. "Why didn't they give him a bed? I bet that ugly hay gave him the itches and made him sneeze!"

I was jolted back to the here and now when Savannah called out, "Look at me, Mom, look at me! Aren't I just lovely?" She was pirouetting down the aisle in her fairy slippers, the price tag still attached. Music from *The Nutcracker* filtered from the intercom.

Coincidence? I thought not.

I pray she keeps this love of finding and wanting beauty in life. I tossed the magical shoes into our shopping cart.

Sensible? Perhaps not. But I had no doubt in my mind—and heart—that it was the right thing, the *lovely* thing to do.

Stephanie Ray Brown

X-Ray Vision

We say "I love you" to our children, but it's not enough. Maybe that's why mothers hug and hold and rock and kiss and pat.

Joan McIntosh

One day, I was cleaning and reorganizing my dresser drawers. My three-year-old helper carried pile after pile and placed them at the foot of the bed. T-shirts, underwear and shirts awaited sorting and refolding. She peered into each drawer to make certain I had emptied everything.

In the bottom of Daddy's dresser, Christina spotted a large manila envelope. As she toddled over to the bed to carefully place it next to the growing mound of clothes, curiosity got the better of her.

"Mommy, what's this?" She flipped it end-over-end.

"It's an X-ray, honey."

"What's an X-ray, Mommy?"

"It's a picture of the inside of someone's body."

"Oh. Can I see the inside of someone's body?"

"Sure, sweetie. Here, let me take it out and show you how to look at it."

With her blonde pigtails bouncing, she carried the envelope to me and watched as I unwound the string that latched it. Eagerly, she pulled the top edge open to peer inside.

"Gentle now, we don't want to damage the picture," I warned.

Her bare feet danced on the golden carpet. She shook with Christmas-like excitement as I pulled the film from its protective covering.

"Let me see. Let me see."

"Calm down, and I'll show you." I sat on the floor, faced the window and patted the rug next to me. "First, we have to hold the picture up to the light, like this."

A small frown creased her forehead as she strained to make sense of what she saw. "I can't find the picture."

"Sweetie, it's the inside of my body," I stressed. "It shows bones. Look. Here. This is my backbone." I traced the thick column in the center. "And you see this? This is you!"

"That's me?" Her brows furrowed, and she tilted her head from side to side.

"It sure is, when you were a baby." I pointed and traced the outlines to help her understand. "Up here is your head, and this is your back—just like mine, but very small."

"Ohhh . . ." Christina leaned close and examined every detail.

"And see this? This is your leg, and this is your arm. What do you think about that?"

Christina pondered the question for a minute, then turned to me with a huge smile. "Mommy, we were bones together!"

She pushed aside the picture and gave me a tight squeeze, locking forever our sacred bond.

Jo Moon

off the mark
by Mark Parisi
www.offthemark.com
BEFORE SHE WAS BORN, I GOT TO SEE HER ULTRASOUND... NOW I GET TO HEAR IT...
WAAA
offthemark.com
©2003 MARK PARISI, DIST. BY UFS, INC.
MarkParisi@aol.com 1-24
MARK PARISI

Paying the Price

There I was, standing in the rain and mud under the tall evergreen behind our house, holding Cissy's hand and hoping we didn't catch cold. I thought about our trip to the pet store.

I had narrowed down her options: She couldn't have a dog because the landlord wouldn't allow it. She couldn't have a cat because I was allergic. She couldn't have a hamster-mouse-gerbil because I couldn't stand the smell of cages or the thought of one of them getting out. She couldn't have fish because I didn't want to clean an aquarium.

Still, she found herself a little critter to love. And really, I kind of loved it, too.

It was exotic, a beautiful specimen: a Chinese Firebelly Toad. Loving it already, Cissy named it Lucy and dug all of her change out of her jacket pocket to pay for it. Exactly $1.46 short, she looked at me pleadingly, and I forked over the extra money.

Lucy was dark green with bright orange spots, and she didn't croak or bite or smell funny or anything obnoxious. She just hopped around her little habitat cage and ate flies. She wasn't bumpy or warty or ugly or suffering from an overactive bladder like the toads we used to find in my grandma's garden when we were kids. She looked more like a frog than a toad, and most importantly, my daughter loved her.

Every day, Cissy scampered to the windowsills to search for flies. She fed the toad and talked to it, and most strangely, gave it an occasional ride in her Barbie Corvette. No toad ever had it so good.

But one morning a few months later, I discovered something terrible. Lucy was very still and very quiet.

The mother in me wanted to protect my little girl from the shock of losing her dear little amphibious friend. I wanted to run to the pet store, buy another Lucy and replace the creature before my daughter noticed. But it was too late.

Cissy woke and ran to feed Lucy. But Lucy wouldn't move. "Is Lucy sleeping, Mommy?" she asked.

"No," I said, patting Cissy's head and hugging her. "I'm afraid Lucy died."

She stared at the toad as if she could somehow will it awake. Her bottom lip jutted out and trembled as she whimpered, "W-w-will Lucy go to heaven?"

I felt heartsick as I tried to reassure her.

And so, there we stood later that dreary afternoon, out in the rain . . . at a Chinese Firebelly Toad's funeral. We'd placed Lucy in an old ring box, tied it closed with a ribbon and dug a small hole back under the evergreen tree where we knew no one would mow over her grave.

Sobbing, Cissy tenderly put the small box in the ground, and together we patted muddy dirt over the top.

Out of her pocket, she pulled a smooth oval stone and set it gently on the mound.

In orange-marker scribble, it simply said, "I Love Lucy."

And I shed a few tears of my own as I witnessed my four-year-old's first painful lesson about life and love and loss.

Autumn Conley

A Higher Plane

Children are not things to be molded, but are people to be unfolded.

Jess Lair

I found it today—the papier-mâché airplane Matt made so long ago. He was in kindergarten then. Now both Matt and Mike are grown, and I've been going through their outgrown treasures.

Memories flooded back as I looked at Matt's plane. He'd spent many mornings in the basement by himself. First, he rolled newspaper to form the wings and body. He used half a roll of masking tape to fasten them together before he mixed the wallpaper paste, stirring so no lumps would spoil the finished plane. And he didn't tear the newspaper strips; he cut them.

Matt waited three days for the plane to dry. He dribbled a little when he painted it, but the red and yellow mixed together made a nice camouflage-orange. We discussed the propeller, and he finally decided to cut blades from a margarine tub lid. Fastened in place, the propeller would "really spin."

At last the airplane was finished, and he decided to take it for show-and-tell that very day.

As the morning progressed, his confidence in the idea faded. "Will the kids think it's dumb?"

I tried to reassure him, but perhaps because he'd had to ask for it, he thought my praise was insincere. Shortly before lunch, he told me he didn't think he'd show the plane after all, and he set it down on the dining room table.

It was still there when third-grader Mike came home for lunch and examined it. "Hey, Matt, this is neat."

"Ya really think so?" asked Matt, who thought his older brother knew everything.

"Yup."

Nothing more was said about it while the boys ate their lunch, but when they left for school, I noticed Matt carrying his plane. Mike's simple, unsolicited praise assured Matt the plane was really good and boosted his self-esteem.

Now, I realize my grown sons probably don't even recall the papier-mâché plane, but I tuck it carefully back into the drawer to remind me of the power of praise.

Ellen Javernick

Cookie Cutter Connection

*Let me not forget that I am the daughter of a
woman . . . who herself never ceased to flower,
untiringly, during three quarters of a century.*

Colette

I couldn't remember exactly how we'd made them—
just that it was sort of like making cookies: rolling the
dough, cutting the shapes, baking the ornaments. All I
knew was that this Christmas my preschool daughters
were dexterous enough to create the kind of ornaments I
used to make with my own mother when I was a little girl.

The thought brought an extra twinge of loneliness as I
faced this first holiday season without Mom and the real-
ization that I couldn't just call her for the recipe we'd used.

After tossing and turning in bed one night, I crept from
its warmth to the chill of the basement. I dug through a
box of my mom's possessions—tattered letters, greeting
cards, photographs. At the bottom I found what I'd been
searching for: her cookbook. The cover was faded with
age, the spine ripped from years of use.

Yellowed newspaper clippings and recipes torn from

magazines fluttered to my lap as I thumbed the pages. There! At the back—in Mom's own handwriting—I discovered a small sheet of paper titled, "Dough Ornaments." With moist eyes, I traced my fingers over the words, feeling a connection. Satisfied, I returned to bed.

Tomorrow, I'll share a bit of my mom with the girls. I drifted to sleep with a sense of peace and determination.

The next day, with Mom's favorite Christmas CD filling the room, the girls and I went to work. Rolling. Cutting. Baking. *How I wish Mom could share this moment,* I thought.

Our first batch, we decided, would make nice gifts for friends and relatives. My three-year-old thoughtfully held up an ornament in the shape of an angel. "Mommy, this one's for Grandma."

The familiar ache of Mom's death knotted my throat and my heart.

"Grandma's in heaven," my four-year-old announced. "You can't give her an ornament."

"That's okay," she shrugged. "I'll just hang it *way* up high on the tree so Grandma can see it from heaven."

I couldn't stifle the tears any longer as I wrapped my daughters in a tight hug. Together, we went to the tree and hung the angel on the very tallest branch we could find. And I smiled at the ornament the girls and I had crafted.

A legacy. Mother-to-daughter.

Tessa Floehr

Weavings

*If you've ever had a mother, and if she's given
you and meant to you all the things you care for
most, you never get over it.*

Anne Douglas Sedgwick

With mere minutes left, I fumble in front of the bathroom mirror to make myself look presentable enough to
drive to preschool. Damp clumps of hair fall into my eyes
as I quickly rub moisturizer over my cheeks. Still, I can't
resist when one of my twin daughters runs into the bathroom and asks, "Can you braid my hair, Mommy?"

I smile into the mirror. Braids are Elise's latest obsession.

"Okay, but we need to hurry. We don't have much time
today."

Elise jumps onto her little bathroom stool, straightens
her back, lifts her chin and stares into the bathroom mirror, eagerly waiting for my fingers to transform her long,
dark blonde hair.

I can relate to my three-and-a-half-year-old's love of
twisted tresses. My own kindergarten photo shows blonde
braids stretching below my shoulders. A few contrary

strands are unraveled, but I'm smiling with my tongue pressed slightly between all the spaces in my front teeth. I went to school with my hair in braids almost every day that year.

"I want *two* braids, Mommy," says Elise, emphasizing her request by forming her little fingers into a "v."

I open the top bathroom drawer filled to the rim with every hair accessory imaginable: crocheted headbands, sparkly barrettes and a rainbow of grosgrain ribbons. I grab the hot pink comb from the top of the heap and begin wrestling morning tangles from Elise's hair with one hand while plunging my other to the bottom of the drawer.

"Why don't I ever organize this mess?" I feel around for two small rubber bands. "Ahh ... got 'em!" I say with exaggerated excitement to distract Elise from the tugs of my comb. She winces but keeps still. Even at such a young age, she is willing to forgo some comfort for beauty.

I hold each band between my teeth for quick retrieval. "Okay, Ellie," I mumble through clenched jaws, "time to keep very still."

It isn't until I begin braiding that I realize *why* I love my kindergarten photo so much. The photo reminds me of treasured times when my mom gave me her undivided attention. We'd talk about what I would do at school that day or what she would do at work. At times, we were silent, simply enjoying the quiet morning ritual. While she wove my hair, Mom was all mine.

As I part Elise's hair, I remember the feel of the comb's teeth moving down the middle of my own scalp and tickling the nape of my neck. Today, Elise's part veers a bit toward her right ear, but it will do.

Sticking the comb under my armpit, I gather the left side of her hair and divide it into three sections. My hands instinctually weave clumps one over the other, over the other, over the other. My joints pop and crack with each movement, just like my mom's used to do, not flexible enough for such nimble needs in the early morning.

"Ouch!" Elise exclaims as I pull the braid tighter to her head. She scrunches her eyebrows in an expression exactly like the one I'd flash my mom in the old gold-rimmed mirror that hung in the only bathroom in our house.

"I'm sorry, honey." I kiss Elise's temple. "Why don't you tell me who you'll play with at school today."

The distraction works. She smiles and quickly begins listing classmates as the braid grows longer and slimmer. I reach the curly ends and retrieve one damp rubber band from my lips to secure my macramé. Elise runs her fingers along the bumpy row of silky knots.

"So beautiful, Mommy." She giggles into the mirror and bounces up and down excitedly. I crack my knuckles and repeat the process on the other side, making sure the final braid falls evenly before securing it.

With pure satisfaction, Elise twists her head back and forth so the stiff ropes slap the side of her face. I remember doing that, too. I look at the clock.

"Whoops, we're going to be late! Go get your shoes on so we can get going." I lift Elise off the step stool. She gives me a quick hug and runs off, her braids bouncing on her shoulders.

Elise is simply happy to have her braids. But today, I sense life's cycle evolving, and I treasure these moments when childhood and motherhood are woven together like the silky skeins of blonde hair.

Karen Olson Burkhartzmeyer

More Chicken Soup?

Many of the stories and poems you have read in this book were submitted by readers like you who had read earlier *Chicken Soup for the Soul* books. We publish at least five or six *Chicken Soup for the Soul* books every year. We invite you to contribute a story to one of these future volumes.

Stories may be up to twelve hundred words and must uplift or inspire. You may submit an original piece, something you have read or your favorite quotation on your refrigerator door.

To obtain a copy of our submission guidelines and a listing of upcoming *Chicken Soup* books, please write, fax or check our Web site.

Please send your submissions to:

Web site: *www.chickensoup.com*
Chicken Soup for the Soul
P.O. Box 30880, Santa Barbara, CA 93130
fax: 805-563-2945

We will be sure that both you and the author are credited for your submission.

For information about speaking engagements, other books, audiotapes, workshops and training programs, please contact any of our authors directly.

Supporting Mothers of Preschoolers Around the World

The world of a mother of preschoolers is a place where doubt, fear, frustration and exhaustion collide with love, joy, hope and elation. It's a turbulent time for both mother and child, and a critical one, as well. The early formative years of children set the stage and tone for their future growth and development. Moms know this, so they pour themselves into parenting. But who pours themselves into moms? MOPS does.

MOPS® (Mothers of Preschoolers) International is a nonprofit Christian organization that's dedicated to empowering and inspiring women in their journey to be the best parents possible. Our primary tool for doing so is through regular meetings where moms in the community gather together to build friendships, encourage one another and discover practical, proven parenting strategies. More than 4,000 MOPS groups meet in all fifty states and thirty-two other countries. In addition, MOPS publishes a wide range of print and electronic material to further assist mothers in the monumental task of raising tomorrow's leaders today. Contact: MOPS International, (303) 733-5353 or *info@MOPS.org*. Visit our Web site at *www.MOPS.org*.

Who Is Jack Canfield?

Jack Canfield is one of America's leading experts in the development of human potential and personal effectiveness. He is both a dynamic, entertaining speaker and a highly sought-after trainer. Jack has a wonderful ability to inform and inspire audiences toward increased levels of self-esteem and peak performance.

He is the author and narrator of several bestselling audio- and videocassette programs, including *Self-Esteem and Peak Performance, How to Build High Self-Esteem, Self-Esteem in the Classroom* and *Chicken Soup for the Soul—Live*. He is regularly seen on television shows such as *Good Morning America, 20/20* and *NBC Nightly News*. Jack has co-authored numerous books, including the *Chicken Soup for the Soul* series, *Dare to Win* and *The Aladdin Factor* (all with Mark Victor Hansen), *100 Ways to Build Self-Concept in the Classroom* (with Harold C. Wells), *Heart at Work* (with Jacqueline Miller) and *The Power of Focus* (with Les Hewitt and Mark Victor Hansen).

Jack is a regularly featured speaker for professional associations, school districts, government agencies, churches, hospitals, sales organizations and corporations. His clients have included the American Dental Association, the American Management Association, AT&T, Campbell's Soup, Clairol, Domino's Pizza, GE, ITT, Hartford Insurance, Johnson & Johnson, the Million Dollar Roundtable, NCR, New England Telephone, Re/Max, Scott Paper, TRW and Virgin Records. Jack has taught on the faculty of Income Builders International, a school for entrepreneurs.

Jack conducts an annual seven-day Training of Trainers program in the areas of self-esteem and peak performance. It attracts entrepreneurs, educators, counselors, parenting trainers, corporate trainers, professional speakers, ministers and others interested in developing their speaking and seminar-leading skills.

For further information about Jack's books, tapes and training programs, or to schedule him for a presentation, please contact:

Self-Esteem Seminars
P.O. Box 30880
Santa Barbara, CA 93130
phone: 805-563-2935 • fax: 805-563-2945
Web site: *www.jackcanfield.com*

Who Is Mark Victor Hansen?

In the area of human potential, no one is more respected than Mark Victor Hansen. For more than thirty years, Mark has focused solely on helping people from all walks of life reshape their personal vision of what's possible. His powerful messages of possibility, opportunity and action have created powerful change in thousands of organizations and millions of individuals worldwide.

He is a sought-after keynote speaker, bestselling author and marketing maven. Mark's credentials include a lifetime of entrepreneurial success and an extensive academic background. He is a prolific writer with many bestselling books, such as *The One Minute Millionaire, The Power of Focus, The Aladdin Factor* and *Dare to Win*, in addition to the *Chicken Soup for the Soul* series. Mark has made a profound influence through his library of audios, videos and articles in the areas of big thinking, sales achievement, wealth building, publishing success, and personal and professional development.

Mark is the founder of the MEGA Seminar Series. MEGA Book Marketing University and Building Your MEGA Speaking Empire are annual conferences where Mark coaches and teaches new and aspiring authors, speakers and experts on building lucrative publishing and speaking careers. Other MEGA events include MEGA Marketing Magic and My MEGA Life.

He has appeared on television (*Oprah, CNN* and *The Today Show*), in print (*Time, U.S. News & World Report, USA Today, New York Times* and *Entrepreneur*) and on countless radio interviews, assuring our planet's people that "You can easily create the life you deserve."

As a philanthropist and humanitarian, Mark works tirelessly for organizations such as Habitat for Humanity, American Red Cross, March of Dimes, Childhelp USA and many others. He is the recipient of numerous awards that honor his entrepreneurial spirit, philanthropic heart and business acumen. He is a lifetime member of the Horatio Alger Association of Distinguished Americans, an organization that honored Mark with the prestigious Horatio Alger Award for his extraordinary life achievements.

Mark Victor Hansen is an enthusiastic crusader of what's possible and is driven to make the world a better place.

Mark Victor Hansen & Associates, Inc.
P.O. Box 7665
Newport Beach, CA 92658
phone: 949-764-2640
fax: 949-722-6912
Web site: *www.markvictorhansen.com*

Who Is Maria Nickless?

Maria Nickless is the coauthor of the *New York Times* bestseller, *Chicken Soup for the Bride's Soul*. She is also the former Director of Marketing and Public Relations for Chicken Soup for the Soul Enterprises, Inc. Maria oversaw campaigns for over forty-five *Chicken Soup* titles, including successfully orchestrating The Largest Book Signing Event in History in 1998, as recognized by the *Guinness Book of World Records*.

Recently she has begun speaking at bridal shows, sharing the message "You're Not Marrying Your Wedding Day" to brides. Also, continuing in her passion for marketing, Maria hosts workshops and coaches new authors and writers on book marketing.

Prior to working for Chicken Soup for the Soul Enterprises, Inc., Maria was in real-estate development, where she was involved in project management and corporate event programs. Having a passion for event planning, over the years Maria has led community-driven charity events through her local church congregation. She is a member of Leadership Tomorrow, a nonprofit organization designed to empower citizens in their commitment to community service.

Maria resides in southern California with her husband, Ward, and children, Madison and Jack. Maria is also an avid photographer and enjoys antique shopping with her husband. When she's not "busy," Maria loves spending time with her mommy friends and basking in the love of her children as she watches them grow.

If you wish to contact Maria, please e-mail her at *maria@chicken soupforthebridesoul.com* or visit *www.bridesoul.com*.

Who Is Elisa Morgan?

Elisa Morgan is president and CEO of MOPS International, Inc. (*www.mops.org*), based in Denver, Colorado, which provides resources and encouragement to moms of young children.

Her daily radio program, *MOMSense*, is broadcast on more than 700 outlets nationwide. A nationally known speaker, Morgan is also the author of several books, including *Mom to Mom, Meditations for Mothers, Naked Fruit, Mom's Devotional Bible, Twinkle: Sharing Your Faith One Light at a Time* and *The Orchard: A Parable*. She is coauthor with Carol Kuykendall of books such as *What Every Child Needs, What Every Mom Needs, Children Change a Marriage* and *Real Moms*.

Elisa received a B.S. in Psychology from the University of Texas and a Master of Divinity in Counseling from Denver Seminary. She served as Dean of Women at Western Bible College, now Colorado Christian University.

Elisa and her husband, Evan, live with their family in Centennial, Colorado.

Contributors

Kathleen Ahrens is a professor in linguistics at National Taiwan University. She is also a regional advisor for the Society of Children's Book Writers and Illustrators. You can read more about her at *www.kathleenahrens.com*.

Caroline Akervik is a graduate of Bryn Mawr College and holds an M.A. in English from the University of Wisconsin–Eau Claire. The greatest source of joy and inspiration in her life is her family. She also writes romance under the pen name Isabelle Kane. Please visit her Web site at *www.isabellekane.com*.

Linda Carol Apple and her husband, Neal, live in northwest Arkansas along with their children and grandchildren. She is an inspirational writer and speaker. Linda currently speaks for Stonecroft Ministries and is writing a historical fiction novel set during the 1850 Gold Rush. Please visit her Web site at *www.lindacapple.com* or e-mail her at *psalm10218@cox-internet.com*.

Carita Stroble Barlow was born and raised in Boone, Iowa. Obtaining a B.A. degree in Music Education, she has taught in public schools and has maintained a private music studio for twenty years, teaching string instruments. Also a popular piano accompanist, she loves to share her talent and love of music with nursing home residents and anyone who will listen. The mother of five grown children and grandmother of nine, she has lived in Colorado for the past thirty years.

Angie Barr is a stay-at-home mom from Memphis, Tennessee. She enjoys spending time with her daughter, reading, creative writing, shopping, singing and outdoor activities. She plans to continue writing fun stories and poems to share with other moms of preschoolers. Please e-mail her at *cheetahangie@yahoo.com*.

Melissa Blanco is currently a stay-at-home mom to her children, Madison (4) and Peyton (3). She received her bachelor's degree from Gonzaga University in 1996. Melissa enjoys running, scrapbooking and writing. She is continually inspired by her husband and children.

Elaine L. Bridge worked in the woods on the West Coast as a forester before becoming a stay-at-home mom to her three boys. Now living in Ohio, she is devoted to developing her relationship with God, caring for her family and writing inspirational material. Please e-mail her at *lanie0b@brecnet.com*.

Natalie Bright is a freelance writer, and her articles have appeared in several local venues. A creative nonfiction article won Honorable Mention in a *ByLine Magazine* contest. She holds a B.B.A. and lives in Texas with her husband and two sons. She hopes to publish a picture book one day.

Jennifer Brown is a freelance writer whose award-winning fiction, nonfiction and poetry have appeared in over a dozen publications around the world. Jennifer is a graduate of William Jewell College and a happily married stay-at-home mother of three. To contact Jennifer, visit *www.freewebs.com/jennifer_brown*.

Stephanie Ray Brown of Henderson, Kentucky, has learned as a mother not to make a mountain out of a molehill. Children are little for only a short time. She enjoys writing about raising Savannah and Cameron with her husband Terry's help. Her stories have been blessed to be included in over ten anthologies. This Murray State elementary-education grad is currently working on her ultimate dream as a writer and teacher—a children's picture book.

Karen Olson Burkhartzmeyer has a Master of Science in Journalism from Northwestern University and is a former Chicago televison news producer. Now she's a freelance writer and the mom of four-year-old twin girls. Karen, her husband and daughters live in Minneapolis, Minnesota.

Avagail Burton is a full-time animal control officer in Oklahoma. She insists writing is her daily stress relief. She enjoys fishing, camping and boating. She takes a vacation with her son whom she has remained close to, every year on his birthday. She is almost finished with a book on animal control, but enjoys writing short stories. She can be e-mailed at *sean246@webtv.net.*

Cheryl L. Butler is a freelance writer and proud mother of seven children. She is passionate about helping families and educators understand the extreme importance of taking a positive approach when helping children manage and overcome their developmental delays. Cheryl enjoys family time along with walking, scrapbooking and gardening.

Dave Carpenter has been a full-time cartoonist and humorous illustrator since 1981. His cartoons have appeared in *Barrons,* the *Wall Street Journal, Forbes, Better Homes and Gardens, Good Housekeeping, Woman's World, First,* the *Saturday Evening Post* and numerous other publications. Dave can be reached at PO Box 520, Emmetsburg, IA 50536 or by calling 712-852-3725.

Dr. Mary Comeau-Kronenwetter is an Adjunct Assistant Professor of Humanities at Colby-Sawyer College. Previously published work includes journal articles on civic participation, Japanese culture, linguistics and foreign language teaching, and sports education for the physically and developmentally disabled. She lives in New Hampshire with her husband and son.

Autumn Conley is the author of several articles, essays and poems in many notable national and local publications. Her first book, *The Monster's Mind: A Novella,* was released in early 2005, and her second book, *Colby's Peace,* will be released in early 2006. Autumn enjoys writing a monthly column for Sisters in the Lord, mentors young writers, and will be working as co-editor for American Dialogue and Postscripts in 2006. You can contact her at *conleya@cedarville.edu.*

Karna Converse is a full-time mother and part-time freelance writer whose work has been published in several regional publications. She lives in Storm Lake, Iowa, with her husband, Ken, and their three children, who are now fourteen, eleven and nine. Please e-mail her at *conversekj@iw.net.*

Lisa Wood Curry grew up in Chicora, Pennsylvania, graduated from Indiana University of Pennsylvania, and lives near Pittsburgh with her husband, two sons, two dachshunds and two cats. She is a contributor to *Chicken Soup for the Working Woman's Soul* and *Chicken Soup for the Fisherman's Soul.* E-mail Lisa at *lisacurry1@verizon.net.*

Michele Ivy Davis is a freelance writer whose articles have appeared in a variety of magazines as well as in newspapers and law-enforcement publications. Her story, "Diane's Walk," was included in *Chicken Soup for the Sister's Soul.* Michele's award-winning debut novel, *Evangeline Brown and the Cadillac Motel,* was published in 2004 by Dutton, an imprint of Penguin, USA. Learn more about her at *www.MicheleIvyDavis.com.*

Mindy Ferguson writes Bible studies and speaks to women's groups with messages of encouragement and hope. She served as Director of Curriculum

Development at Cy-Fair Christian Church and is the founder of Fruitful Word Ministries. Mindy lives in Houston, Texas, with her husband and two children. Please e-mail her at *mindy@fruitfulword.org.*

Lizann Flatt has been a writer and full-time mom living in Ontario, Canada, since 1997. She often finds herself at soccer fields, hockey and skating arenas, and playgrounds with her husband and three kids. Everyday life often provides inspiration for her writing. She writes short stories and nonfiction books for kids.

Tessa Floehr is a former teacher now devoting her time to raising her two young daughters. She enjoys writing, teaching crafts to children and teaching Sunday School with her husband. She has been involved with her local Mothers of Preschoolers group, creating curriculum and volunteering for MOPPETS. Contact her at *tessa@floehr.com.*

Mandy Flynn is a wife and mother of two living in Albany, Georgia. She began a newspaper career at the age of nineteen and currently writes a Sunday column for *The Albany Herald.* Her book, *Act Like You've Got Some Sense,* was published in 2004. E-mail her at *flyn1862@bellsouth.net.*

Sally Friedman has contributed to national, regional, and local newspapers and magazines, including the *New York Times, Ladies' Home Journal, Family Circle* and *Bride's.* She is happily addicted to chocolate, her three daughters, and her seven beautiful and brilliant grandchildren. E-mail her at *pinegander@aol.com.*

Sheree Rochelle Gaudet, mother of three, has published features and essays on parenting, husband/wife relationships and surviving breast cancer. She enjoys Rollerblading, reading and dancing with her children. She is at work on her first novel. Please e-mail her at *shereegaudet@yahoo.com.*

Cindy Gehl writes parenting-related articles and provides copywriting services to small businesses. She lives in Farmington, Minnesota, with her husband and two very busy little girls. Please e-mail her at *cindy@gehlink.com* or visit her Web site at *gehlink.com.*

Randy Glasbergen is one of America's most widely and frequently published cartoonists. More than 25,2000 of his cartoons have been published by *Funny Times, Harvard Business Review, Cosmopolitan, Good Housekeeping, Medical Economics* and many others. His daily comic panel "The Better Half" is syndicated worldwide by King Features Syndicate. He is also the author of three cartooning instruction books and several cartoon anthologies. To read a new cartoon everyday or order cartoon merchandise please visit Randy's Web site at *444.glasbergen.com.*

Sandra Giordano holds an M.A. in English from William Paterson University and is a member of Sigma Tau Delta, the International English Honor Society. She is a consultant and freelance writer for educational and parenting publications. Her most rewarding job, says Sandra "is being a mommy to Christina and Joey."

Speaker-artist **Bonnie Compton Hanson** is a former editor and author of books for both adults and children, including the popular *Ponytail Girls* series and several teacher's resource books, plus hundreds of published articles and poems. Contact her at 3330 S. Lowell St., Santa Ana, CA 92707; (714) 751-7824; *bonnieh1@ worldnet.att.net.*

Jonny Hawkins loves his two young sons, Nathaniel and Zachary. They often provide hilarious material for the many thousands of his cartoons that have appeared in over 300 magazines, such as *Readers Digest, Guidepost, Natural History* and many others. He lives in Sherwood, Michigan, with his wife, Carissa, and the boys. He can be reached at *jonnyhawkins2nz@yahoo.com.*

Libby Hempen received her Bachelor of Science degree from Texas Christian University in 1990. She is a wife and mother of two preschool boys. She has worked as a flight attendant for fourteen years and enjoys traveling, reading, writing and anything outdoors.

Born in Michigan and raised in Texas, **Renee Hixson** now resides in beautiful British Columbia with her husband and four children. She has taught Sunday School, high-school English and written early childhood educational curriculum. At present, Renee is working on a romantic adventure novel. Please e-mail her at *rhixson@telus.net.*

Rachelle Hughes received a Bachelor of Journalism degree from Brigham Young University in 1996. She freelances for magazines, newspapers and organizations on home design, parenting, art and writing. She has had a children's e-book published, as well as poetry. She enjoys reading, gardening and mothering her three children. Contact her at *thughes@rocketmail.com.*

Tasha Jacobson received her Bachelor of Arts in Health Information Administration from the College of St. Scholastica (Duluth, Minnesota) in 1995. She now resides in Minnetonka, Minnesota, with her high-school sweetheart husband and their three children. Tasha cherishes time spent with family and writing for children.

Ellen Javernick is a first-grade teacher in Loveland, Colorado. She's the author of numerous articles and books for children. She enjoys playing tennis and spending time with her five children and their families. You can reach her at (970) 667-5725.

Brian G. Jett has published works and quotations in the *Chicken Soup for the Soul* series, *The Washington Post* and *Venice Magazine.* He holds honorable mention status with the National Poetry Guild, and he loves being a dad and husband. His Web site is *www.hangtough.com.*

Maureen Johnson received her bachelor's degree from the University of Stirling, Scotland, in 1987. She met her Australian partner in Japan and moved to Sydney in 1991. She has just completed her first young adult novel, *Something More,* and is currently working on her second. E-mail her at *macbethm@optus.net.*

Diane Kagey has been married for twenty-five years and is a mother of five children. She lives in West Linn, Oregon. Diane has a Bachelor of Science degree in Health Science. She enjoys working with children at church, running, cooking, and spending time with friends and family. She can be contacted at *djkagey@comcast.net.*

Libby Kennedy is the proud mother of two preschool graduates. She thinks children should be issued full-body, helmeted, bubble-wrapped jumpsuits. Aside from throwing herself in the path of potentially lethal pathogens (e.g., furry lollipops under the sofa), she writes creative non-fiction and kooky stories for kids. Her e-mail address is *futurehockey@hotmail.com.*

Cheryl Kirking is an author, songwriter and conference speaker who tickles the funny bones and tugs at the heartstrings of audiences nationwide. Her many books include *Crayons in the Dryer: Misadventures and Unexpected Blessings of Motherhood* and *Ripples of Joy.* She is also the mother of triplets. For booking information visit *www.cherylkirking.com.*

Mimi Greenwood Knight is a freelance writer and artist in residence living in Folsom, Lousiana, with her husband, David, and four precious gifts from God:

Haley, Molly, Hewson and Jonah. Her essays and articles have appeared in *Parents, Christian Parenting Today, American Baby, Working Mother, Campus Life, Today's Christian Woman, Sesame Street Parents* and *At-Home Mother*, as well as in anthologies like *Chicken Soup for Every Mom's Soul, A Cup of Comfort for Christians, Lists to Live By* and *Three Ring Circus: How Real Couples Balance Marriage, Work and Family*. She can be reached at *djknight@airmail.net.*

Amy Krause is currently the Director of Special Services in the Missouri public-school system. She lives in Nixa, Missouri, with her husband, Tom, and two boys, Tyler and Sam. You may contact her at *Justmealk@aol.com.*

Jennifer Lawler is the author of more than twenty books, including the *Dojo Wisdom* series (Penguin Compass). She lives in the Midwest with her daughter and two rambunctious dogs. Her Web site is *www.jenniferlawler.com.*

Tanya Lentz, a Utah native, is a wife to Derek and mother of two. She received her B.S. in Marriage, Family and Human Development from Brigham Young University. She plans to write children's books, and is passionate about people, nature and writing. Please e-mail her at *Tanyamlentz@yahoo.com.*

Jaye Lewis is an award-winning writer and contributing author to two *Chicken Soup* books. She lives with her family in the Appalachian Mountains of Virginia. Jaye has completed her first book, which is still looking for a publisher. Jaye's Web site can be found at *www.entertainingangels.org.* E-mail Jaye at *jlewis@smyth.net.*

Karin A. Lovold is a stay-at-home mom to three daughters, ages ten, eight and almost four. She and her husband, Michael, reside in Minnesota where she enjoys writing, reading and hanging out in the woods. She loves writing true stories and many fiction stories as well. Please e-mail her at *kal3860@chartermi.net.*

Donna Lowich received her Master's of Library Science degree from Rutgers University in 1978. She currently works as an information specialist for a nonprofit organization. Besides writing, she enjoys cross-stitch projects featuring cats and Victorian houses.

Myrna C.G. Mibus is a freelance writer and a stay-at-home mom. She lives in Minnesota with her husband and two children. She enjoys quilting, gardening, reading, writing and taking her family flying in her vintage airplane, a 1955 Piper Pacer. E-mail her at *myrnacgmibus@mac.com.*

Lisa Moffitt is a successful business executive, wife and mother of three. She loves to write and speak to women's groups across the country. She uses a blend of humor and charming Southern style to encourage women in all facets of their lives. You can contact her at *LisaMoffitt23@msn.com.*

Maria Monto resides in New Jersey and is the mother of three grown children—Lauren, Andrea and Christopher. She is a travel consultant and has always had a passion for writing. Maria is currently working on a humor collection of both fiction and nonfiction stories and can be e-mailed at *RiaMonto@aol.com.*

Jo Moon grew up in the shadow of the Empire State Building on the New Jersey side of the Hudson River. At age seventeen, she moved with her family to the rocky coast of Maine near Acadia National Park. She owned a women's clothing store for twelve years before changing careers and working for major corporations as Director of International Sales. Her career brought her to the Ozarks where she now resides. An avid traveler, Jo enjoys meeting and writing about the people she encounters.

After brief sojourns in Germany and southern California, **Maryjo Faith Morgan** is immensely grateful to be writing full-time back in Colorado. She enjoys reading (of course!), hiking and tandem biking with her husband, as well as time spent with her now grown son and his family. Contact her at *MaryjoFaithMorgan@hotmail.com*.

Rochelle Nelson speaks nationwide to audiences of women at events and retreats. Rochelle and her husband, Peter, own and operate Nelson Building and Development out of Buffalo, Minnesota, where they also partner in raising their three sons. You can e-mail her at *Rochelle.Nelson@nelsonbuilding.com*.

Marilyn G. Nutter and her husband live in Pennsylvania and have three daughters and a granddaughter. She is a speech-language pathologist; a partner in "Shepherd's Cup," a tea ministry providing inspirational workshops; and a MOPS mentor. Her book, *Dressed Up Moms Devotions to Go*, will be released in 2006. Contact her at *nutter70@comcast.net*.

Eliza Ong received her Bachelor of Arts, with honors, from California University State Northridge. She is an elementary-school teacher in southern California. Eliza enjoys reading, writing, snowboarding, fishing, cooking and spending time with her husband and two children. You can contact her at *jeds)ong@yahoo.com*.

Jennifer Oscar is a former Army officer from Colorado and a graduate of Embry-Riddle Aeronautical University. She and her active-duty husband are busy with Army life and raising their five children. When she isn't keeping track of children, Jennifer is an avid quilter and scrapbooker. She can be e-mailed at *scoilb@hotmail.com*.

Jackie Papandrew is a freelance writer and often harried mom living in Florida. She writes a humor column called *Airing My Dirty Laundry*, using material generously supplied by her family and other assorted ne'er-do-wells. She loves coffee and reading, preferably together. Please e-mail her at *jackie@jackiepapandrew.com*.

Mark Parisi's *Off the Mark* comic panel has been syndicated since 1987 and is distributed by United Media. Mark's humor also graces greeting cards, T-shirts, calendars, magazines (such as *Billboard*), newsletters and books. His cartoons can be found in the pages of many *Chicken Soup for the Soul* books. Lynn is his wife/business partner and their daughter, Jenny, contributes with inspiration (as do three cats).

Sherrie Peterson likes to stay busy. She is an actress, director, producer, writer, inspirational speaker, jewelry designer and mother of two. When she is not traveling doing one of the above, she lives in Boynton Beach, Florida, with her husband, Lee, and their children, Layne and LB. She has her degree in theater from Samford University, but admits that her greatest education in life has come from mothering her two preschoolers. She can be reached at *sherrie@sherriepeterson.com* or *www.sherriepeterson.com*.

Rita M. Pilger has been a stay-at-home mother of five and recently launched a unique new venture as the "Traveling Tea Lady." Rita is an accomplished quilter and avid button collector. She enjoys leisure time with her husband and traveling to visit their two grandchildren. Contact her at *www.travelingtealady.com*.

Kay Conner Pliszka is a frequent contributor to the *Chicken Soup* books, recently winning their 10th Anniversary writing contest. A former teacher and motivational speaker, she is now entertaining audiences with her humorous and inspirational stories. To schedule her for speaking or storytelling engagements, Kay may be reached at *K.Pliszka@prodigy.net*.

Sheri Plucker is a published freelance writer. Her picture book, *Me, Hailey* (Jason and Nordic Publishers), was launched in summer 2005. It explains that children with Down syndrome may look, act and learn differently, but they are special just like you and me. She resides in Snohomish, Washington. Visit her Web site at *www.sheriplucker.com.*

Dan Rosandich is a Michigan based cartoonist who operates his cartoon licensing agency *DansCartoons.com* with clients around the globe. Dan also syndicates the daily cartoon on his homepage, which appears electronically on web sites worldwide. To commission "custom" illustrations or license cartoons, contact Dan at *dan@danscartoons.com.*

Christina Quist is a wife and mom of five children: four boys and one girl, whose ages range from ten to four. Although she holds degrees from various institutions, they serve no practical purpose in the humorous daily activities that she encounters with her family. Please e-mail her at *kcquist@juno.com.*

Author and editor **Carol McAdoo Rehme** recognizes motherhood as her most important calling—it keeps her humble and hopping. Mother of four, she's now the delighted grammy to two. Carol directs a nonprofit, Vintage Voices, Inc., which brings interactive programming to the vulnerable elderly. Contact her at *carol@rehme.com; www.rehme.com.*

Stephen D. Rogers is a stay-at-home dad. While he doesn't get out much, you can always find him at *www.stephendrogers.com.*

Jodi Seidler is the creator of *www.makinglemonade.com* (a network for single parents), a writer, single parent expert and media personality. She has coauthored a girlfriend's guidebook for single and stepmothers, and a book of poetry for the hormonally challenged romantic. Most importantly, she is the single mother of Sam, who is now sixteen.

Sarah Smiley is the author of *Shore Duty*, a syndicated newspaper column, and of the book *Going Overboard* (Penguin/New American Library). To contact Sarah, please visit *www.SarahSmiley.com.*

Christine M. Smith is the mother of three, grandmother of twelve and a foster parent. She enjoys writing anecdotes about her family and friends. She believes there is no greater joy in life than sharing her faith in God and to see it reflected in those she loves. E-mail her at *iluvmyfamilyxxx000@yahoo.com.*

Marsha Smith attended college of the Albemarle. She worked with a national television network for over twenty years. While there, she received the President's Award for Excellence twice and earned her certification in Data Management, She has been published by Blue Mountain Arts and continues to write poetry and short stories. She is currently working on a devotional book for women. She enjoys spending time with her grandchildren and working in her flower garden.

Andrea Stark lives in West Des Moines, Iowa, with her husband and three children. She has been an English teacher, a children's pastor and a full-time homemaker. She plans to spend the rest of her life learning, teaching and writing.

Amanda L. Stevens is an exhausted mother of three preschool-aged children. She is a freelance writer and can be found in various places in print and on the Internet. She is an advocate for autism. Please e-mail her at: *amandalstevens@gmail.com.*

Tsgoyna Tanzman is a freelance writer and author of several children's stories. Tsgoyna resides with her husband and daughter in Palos Verdes, California. When she is not carpooling, she volunteers her time as a Speaker/Child Safety Educator. Additionally, she directs "Characters Come Alive," a program bringing historical characters to life, in elementary classrooms.

Patricia E. Van West, Ed.D., has authored a children's picture book, *The Crab Man* (Turtle Books), and over 100 magazine and newspaper articles. She was born in Amsterdam, the Netherlands, but now lives in exotic central Illinois. She teaches college-level creative writing and can be contacted at *pvanwest@voortrek.com*.

Linda Vujnov is a freelance writer who resides in Orange County, California. As the mother of four children ages two to twelve and a fourteen-year marriage, she is able to gather many amusing stories through her daily experiences. She is currently working on a humorous devotional for moms.

Kristin Walker is a freelance writer and a stay-at-home mom. Her three sons, Noah, Logan and Ethan, constantly inspire her writing and her role as Fixer of All Things Smashed, Stained or Smelly. She lives happily with them and her husband, Sean, in Oswego, Illinois.

June Williams has worked as a waitress, florist, clerk and writer, but she enjoys being a mom best. June lives in Brush Prairie, Washington, with her husband, Mac, where they enjoy the company of their three grandchildren.

Emily O. Wilson received her Bachelor of Arts in English at the University of Texas at San Antonio. She is the mother of two children and is very involved in a Mothers of Preschoolers group at her church. She enjoys photography, scrapbooking, journaling, volunteering and being with her family.

Leslie Wilson, wife to Bret and mother to Charlie, Molly and Reese, writes a weekly humor column, "Reality Motherhood," for *Star Community Newspapers* in Dallas. She speaks to thousands of preschool moms each year at MOPS, ECPTAs, Hearts at Home and Home Front Conferences. Contact her through her Web site at *www.RealityMotherhood.com*.

Gloria Wooldridge resides in Atlantic, Canada, with her husband and two daughters. She works part-time as an education assistant and is involved in facilitating a small-group ministry for women in her local church.

Kris Yankee received her Bachelor of Arts from the University of Michigan in 1990. Mother of two young boys, she enjoys gardening, reading and spending time with her family. In her spare time, Kris is working on several women's fiction novels. Please e-mail her at *kyankee1@yahoo.com*.

On a Role. Reprinted by permission of Linda Rose Vujnov. ©2004 Linda Rose Vujnov.

The Sound of Silence. Reprinted by permission of Mandy Flynn. ©2002 Mandy Flynn.

Seasonal Secrets. Reprinted from Heartbeats. ©2000 by Sandra Byrd. Used by permission of Waterbrook Press, Colorado Springs, CO. All rights reserved.

Hand and Heart. Reprinted by permission of Elaine L. Bridge. ©2001 Elaine L. Bridge.

Holding On. Reprinted by permission of Cheryl Kirking. ©1999 Cheryl Kirking.

A Little Help Please. Reprinted by permission of Mary Elizabeth Hempen. ©2005 Mary Elizabeth Hempen.

Daddy Bear. Reprinted by permission of Melissa Marie Blanco. ©2005 Melissa Marie Blanco.

Oh, What a Ride! Reprinted by permission of Sally Friedman. ©2005 Sally Friedman.

Bee Attitude. Reprinted by permission of Andrea Leigh Stark. ©2005 Andrea Leigh Stark.

Bearing Thanksgiving. Reprinted by permission of Judith M. Lewis. ©2002 Judith M. Lewis.

Of Two Minds. Reprinted by permission of Carol D. Rehme. ©2003 Carol D. Rehme.

Meeting Jeanie. Reprinted by permission of Tanya Marie Lentz. ©2005 Tanya Marie Lentz.

The Grill Drill. Reprinted by permission of Jennifer Marie Brown. ©2005 Jennifer Marie Brown.

Spiced Up. Reprinted by permission of Marilyn Grace Nutter. ©2005 Marilyn Grace Nutter.

When I'm a Grown-Up. Reprinted by permission of Jody Seidler. ©1999 Jody Seidler.

Cents and Sensitivity. Reprinted by permission of Tasha Marie Jacobson. ©2005 Tasha Marie Jacobson.

Picking and Choosing. Reprinted by permission of Jennifer L. Lawler. ©2005 Jennifer L. Lawler.

Marker Magic. Reprinted by permission of Kathleen V. Ahrens and Tracy Love-Geffen. ©2005 Kathleen V. Ahrens and Tracy Love-Geffen.

Back-to-School Q&A. Reprinted by permission of Sarah R. Smiley. ©2004 Sarah R. Smiley.

Growing Up. Reprinted by permission of Marsha Brickhouse Smith. ©2004 Marsha Brickhouse Smith.

Preschool Pangs. Reprinted by permission of Kristine Marie Yankee. ©2005 Kristine Marie Yankee.

Fears and Tears. Reprinted by permission of Elizabeth Kennedy. ©2004 Elizabeth Kennedy.

Late Bloomers. Reprinted by permission of Cheryl L. Butler. ©2005 Cheryl L. Butler.

Mommy's Help, Er. Reprinted by permission of Patricia E. Van West. ©1995 Patricia E. Van West.

Special Delivery. Reprinted by permission of Carita Stroble Barlow. ©2005 Carita Stroble Barlow.